KATE BUSH

A VISUAL DOCUMENTARY BY KEVIN CANN & SEAN MAYES

Omnibus Press

London/New York/Sydney/Cologne

*To my mother, for being a friend —
love Sean.*

To Brigitte — with love, Kevin.

ACKNOWLEDGEMENTS

The authors would like to extend their thanks to: Neville Williams and Jon Bishop of *Cariad Kate* fanzine for all their help and encouragement. Both Neville and Jon put up with our constant calls at all hours and unselfishly opened their files for us. They also introduced us to the invaluable Peter Swales interview with Kate, Paddy and Del Palmer, which appeared in its entirety in *Cariad Kate*. Thanks to Peter for letting us use extended extracts, also Margaret Rose, Sharon and Chris at Chapel Studio, Lindsay Kemp, Bexleyheath Information Centre, Mike Scott – Chief Librarian at Bexley Local Studies Dept., Erith Technical College, *Sounds, Melody Maker, Record Mirror* and *New Musical Express*, Kerry Juby's *In Other Words Kate Bush* radio broadcast, *Homeground* for an excellent publication, Mike Smith, Greg Vandike, Jamie Amos, Philip Norris, Rikki Beadle-Blair for inspiration, Geoff Portass and Roy Puddefoot for their vivid account of 'Experiment IV', Geoff Felix for a guiding hand, Michael Dotchin for 'Babooshka', Tom Robinson for the low-down on EMI, Simon Woods for moral support and John Richardson for putting the authors in touch in the first place.

© Copyright 1988 Omnibus Press
(A Division of Book Sales Limited)

Edited by Chris Charlesworth
Book Designed by Kevin Cann,
Stuart Young, Marc Abbott
(Cipher Design)
Picture Research by Kevin Cann
and Mary McCartney
Project and typesetting co-
ordinated by Caroline Watson

ISBN 0.7119.1039.1
Order No: OP44122

Exclusive distributors:

Book Sales Limited
8/9 Frith Street,
London W1V 5TZ, UK

Music Sales Corporation
24 East 22nd Street,
New York, NY 10010, USA

Music Sales Pty Limited
120 Rothschild Avenue,
Rosebery, NSW 2018, Australia

To the Music Trade only:
Music Sales Limited,
8/9 Frith Street,
London W1V 5TZ, UK

Picture credits:
Gered Mankowitz, Barry Plummer,
BBC Hulton Picture Library,
Syndication International, London
Features International, Universal
Pictorial Press, Daily Express,
Topham Observer Colour Library,
Tom Sheehan, David Redfern,
Bexley Library, Pictorial Press,
Roy Puddefoot, Julie Angel and
Pete Still.

Typeset by Capital Setters,
London. Printed by Scotprint,
Musselburgh, Scotland.

INTRODUCTION

Kevin Cann

On the edge of London's sprawling south-eastern suburbs is a rambling but comfortable farmhouse half-hidden behind old barns and ivy-covered trees. This acre of magic, surrounded by a wooden fence, is where Kate Bush grew up, her imagination stimulated by an eccentric but loving family. Here she discovered Gandalf and Peter Pan, sixties pop bands and Oscar Wilde. Her father played classical piano, and her older brothers introduced her to Irish folk music, mysticism, paganism and poetry.

Kate has always managed to retain the magic of her childhood – it touches all her work. Six years after 'Wuthering Heights' first took her to success and stardom, she built a modern high-tech recording studio in one of the old barns. From this studio came her most searing, soul-searching album, 'Hounds Of Love'.

Last year she made a video for her most recent single, 'Experiment IV', featuring the 'Thing', a sound monster snarling a fatal scream. Three 'monster specialists' took their designs to the farm and were surprised when Kate herself opened the gate and led them into the barn-studio. She made them tea and chatted away, taking an eager interest in their work. As one of them said later, "She's the nicest pop star anyone could want to meet."

Kate Bush is a very special artist who has captured the imagination of a legion of fans over the past 10 years, pursuing her own concerns at her own pace. Taking up to three years to record an album, she regards the blank tape as her canvas, 'painting' vivid sound-pictures of emotions, dreams and states of mind. Kate has become a brilliant virtuoso of the recording studio itself. She uses her extraordinary voice and the talents of carefully chosen musicians to create tone-poems which work directly on the senses, reinforcing the meaning of her words and evoking the feeling of soul speaking to soul. In the intimacy of her studio she loses her inhibitions, 'psyching' herself up to do a vocal with the right emotional feeling.

This book takes you from the days of Kate's magical childhood, through her early success, right up to the present, on the eve of the release of her sixth album. We examine every record, tracing ideas which she has been developing ever since the seeds were first planted. Drawing on interviews with Kate, her family and the people who have worked with her, we follow her progress as writer, singer, record producer, video maker and performer.

We hope to dispel some of the mystery of both her life and her music without spoiling any of the magic. The more we have learned the more fascinating she becomes.

This year marks Kate Bush's thirtieth birthday and we would like this book to celebrate the life and work of this unique artist.

'We put this moment . . . here.'

Sean Mayes/Kevin Cann July 1988

LFI

INDEX

THE BUSH FAMILY

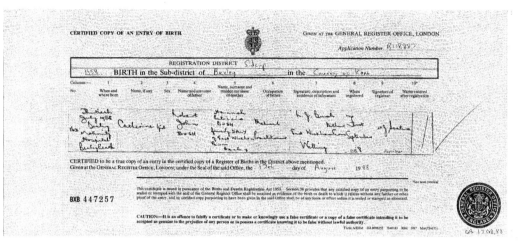

1958

30th July 1958. Catherine Bush born at Bexleyheath Maternity Hospital, South East London. A daughter to Dr Robert John Bush, originally from South Ockendon, and Hannah Bush (née Daly), from County Waterford, Ireland. A sister to John Carder Bush (Jay), born: 1944, and Paddy Bush, born: 1952.

Born into a musical family, Kate was to grow up listening to a mix of traditional Irish and old English folk and contemporary rock. This unusual mix, a legacy of her two brothers, was to be one of the main inspirations for her own unique creativity. Her eldest brother Jay, a published and accomplished poet, helped to develop Kate's own artistic interests.

"I think we are an exceptionally close family. Without my family I wouldn't be where I am today."

Like most attractive goals, fame brings with it benefits and problems. For some it becomes a burden too overpowering to handle, for others, the glory and reward of dreams and years of effort. For a few artists the glory is not the fame or the fortune, but the opportunity to pursue their creative talent without let or hindrance. This talent, in the case of Kate Bush, was impressive enough to inspire nationwide attention overnight, capturing hearts and imaginations with her unique vocal delivery and beautiful windswept looks. When Kate Bush arrived it was certainly in style.

By its very nature popular music rewards the young, as it is mainly the young who vote by buying records. At 19, Kate Bush could have been forgiven for falling in the deep end under the intense media gaze. Her first single 'Wuthering Heights' remains her biggest hit single to date. Responding like a seasoned professional twice her age, she conducted herself in interviews and personal appearances with a maturity very few teenagers could offer. It was clear from day one that Kate Bush was more special than most.

If stars are born and not made, then perhaps we should consider Kate Bush in that light. Family and upbringing not only helped prepare Kate for a rich and varied life, they unwittingly fuelled her future talents.

Kate was born the youngest child of Robert and Hannah Bush on July 30 1958 at Bexleyheath Maternity Hospital. A few days later she was brought to the nearby home in East Wickham, a beautiful farm house where she would grow up and ultimately consider 'home'. It was large and mysterious with plenty of space for a fertile imagination to develop.

A school friend of Kate's once described the home as 'very sort of wooden with too many rooms'. The interior was always homely and well ordered (apart from Kate and Paddy's bedrooms which were usually in a mess); Mrs Bush kept her home spotless and well polished. The building's splendid oak beams which provide the backbone of the 350-year-old house were originally salvaged from scrapped 'Men Of War' ships from Woolwich dockyard; the very soul of East Wickham farm's rustic beauty.

Kate's brothers, John Carder (nicknamed Jay) and Paddy were born in 1944 and 1952 respectively. When Kate was a child the family emigrated to Australia but returned less than a year later to the familiar surroundings of East Wickham farm. Little is known about this period in Kate's life, or why the family decided to emigrate from such idyllic surroundings. Kate's only mention of it was in a *Flexi-pop* magazine piece entitled 'Testament Of Youth': "For about six months I went to Australia with my parents. I was

only five or six. I met a kangaroo and that was really beautiful. And my brother met an emu. The emu freaked out."

Kate's childhood years were spent much the same as any other girl who enjoyed a happy and secure family unit. Her family were wealthy, creatively as well as financially, and lived comfortably. A schoolfriend would later say of Kate: "She just asked for money and got it, whenever she wanted."

Dr Bush would often leave his loose change lying around the house and Kate would be allowed to dip into this whenever she needed. When she was younger she would hide her money in the mouth of the lionskin rug in the front room. Kate simply grew up accustomed to money but never boasted of her family's wealth. Once, schoolfriends passing by her house en route to the cinema were amazed when they were told little Catherine Bush lived there.

The large, tree-lined house was the ideal retreat for the unusually talented Bush family, and friends would later recall how the Bush home was always ringing to the sound of music, mostly supplied by Paddy playing his collection of stringed instruments, or Robert Bush playing piano. Often, Dr Bush would practise for hours at a time on the main piano, filling the house with Chopin, Beethoven and Schubert. Occasionally he would accompany Kate while she studied for school violin exam pieces: "In 20 minutes she would know them by heart, put the fiddle away and start improvising on the piano," he later recalled.

1963/64

1963/64. The Bush family emigrate to Australia, an experiment which wasn't to last and within a year they were once more home at East Wickham farm.

Bexleyheath Maternity Hospital where it all began. Kate was born in this building on July 30th 1958. The maternity hospital has since become the headquarters of the Bexleyheath area health authority. Situated at the western end of Lavernock Road, the building is very much as it was when Kate was born.

Kevin Cann

Kate would often join Paddy on old English folk songs like those sung by A.L. Lloyd, one of Paddy's favourites. "I was brought up on traditional folk music, mostly Irish stuff, and that must be the biggest influence on me I suppose, because I grew up with it. Bert Lloyd is the man as far as I'm concerned," she has said. In 1986 Kate recorded a song once covered by Lloyd, 'The Handsome Cabin Boy'. Kate had chosen Lloyd's version for her 'All Time Top Ten' list broadcast by Radio One in 1980.

From an early age the pure, traditional inflections of simple Irish and English ballads engrained their invisible rhythms on young Cathy, the importance of which can be traced through to her musical output today. Later Kate recalled of her household: "Music was an obsession." And, as the obsession became more and more creative, so actual songs began to take shape. "Music and words used to come together at the same time. There's something warm and friendly in music."

All of Kate's family have expressed a creative edge to some degree. In the late sixties Jay was known as a reasonably successful poet. He gave readings of his work on the radio, published a slim volume of poetry entitled *The Creation Edda* (in an edition of 100 by the Sceptre Press) and had work published in *Poetry Review*. Jay was the earliest and possibly the most important influence on Kate's writing, introducing her to major interests like Greek mythology and Gurdjieff's mysticism which Kate devoured enthusiastically.

Paddy is also an accomplished musician with a substantial collection of unusual and rare musical instruments and his search for new sounds fascinated Kate. In later years his contributions to Kate's LPs would be remarkably varied: mandolin, balalaika, sitar, koto, harmonica, violin, dijeridu and even a musical saw!

Kate's father introduced her to the piano. When Paddy required someone to accompany him regularly while he played violin, Kate was the natural choice. Dr Bush showed Kate the first few keys and very soon she was creating chords and simple melodies. Kate had already been studying the violin at school and with a private teacher. Although not really enjoying the instrument, it was compulsory at her school to learn an instrument, but she dropped the violin in favour of the piano as soon as her mother allowed her. After her first year at St. Joseph's Grammar school she was listed 'Grade 2' at violin, not bad for an instrument in which she had little interest.

Privately, Kate would practise keyboards away from the farm house in an outbuilding which was once a Victorian wash house. In there was an old church organ with a foot pump which provided a home for families of mice. In the same building, John Bush would often rehearse his own folk band. Intuitively, Cathy would join in on choruses, and jig along to the music.

From early on in Kate's life it was obvious to her family that she was to be a gifted musician. As her father later revealed in a rare interview; "Her songs seem to write themselves, whole stanzas at a time, in her head, while I'm struggling to put one word after the next." At 13, Cathy Bush wrote the outline to one of her most endearing future hits, 'The Man With The Child In His Eyes'.

The family bond was, and still is, an incredibly strong one, a symbiotic relationship which particularly rubbed off on Kate. Each and every influence was absorbed and filed accordingly, but at first there was nothing to indicate that Kate would be anything more than just a pretty and intelligent girl. She would later amaze schoolfriends when she suddenly burst, unannounced, to the top of the music scene.

Only recently has another fascinating side of Kate's childhood been revealed in a book entitled *Cathy*, produced and published by John Carder Bush. The book shows young Kate with the genuine look of prodigy in her eyes. At a time when schoolfriends remember Kate to have been shy and timid, her brother's camera reveals nothing but maturity and poise. The book's 29 black and white photographs often show her in historical costumes chosen by her brother, and make-shift get-ups often sizes too big for her. Long summer weekends and after-school evenings are rediscovered and carefully described by John Bush:

"Thinking, dreaming, hoping, waiting patiently, Cathy was never hurried. Patience usually comes with experience but she was born with it and it is a great gift to have. The sleepy brown eyes and the unkempt hair hint at a nostalgia for lakes and the occasional plop of a trout, and the wild glamour of Irish music. You can see other little Cathies looking just like this one on the streets of Galway."

John Bush's book is a beautiful record of his little sister's magical qualities, a clear vision of things to come. A rare glimpse into the outbuildings and gardens of her childhood, the very essence of a chapter Kate has not altogether closed. Perhaps 'the woman with the child in her eyes?'

1967

1967. Kate attends St. Joseph's Prep School, situated alongside the grammar school she would later attend.

Right: *Mrs Bush, Paddy, Kate and Jay relax with a hound of love.*

BBC

8

Life in the Bush household was generally no different from other average middle class English families. Kate's mother ran a smooth and efficient home, giving Kate and her brothers plenty of space to 'do their own thing', only occasionally commenting on the state of their dress. A school friend of Kate's later remarked, "Her mother always seemed to be around but didn't seem to tell Kate what to do." This attitude was also adopted by Dr Bush, and Kate and her friends would have the run of the large house and grounds without restriction.

Bexley Local Studies Dept.

Left: *East Wickham Farm c.1920.*

Like most children Kate was fond of pets. She kept hamsters, cats and a rabbit, which she would often let out for friends. But feminine interests like Wendy houses never really took her fancy. Most young girls dream of owning a large and private Wendy house, Kate possessed a purpose-built Tudor style house but rarely went inside. Instead she preferred to play around the rest of the farm, in its large inviting barn, one of the out-houses or in her private little den within the main house, a room that was hers in addition to her bedroom. When other members of the household were out, Kate and friends would prepare feasts in the kitchen, then disappear to her room to devour them (when they were good enough to eat that was!). Other times would be spent roasting marshmallows over the fire in her room, invariably burning them and stinking the place out.

Her little room in the house was all-important to her. The floor was littered with cushions, records, books and magazines and was in a constant state of disarray. There she could play records from her brothers' collections by the likes of The Incredible String Band, Bob Dylan and The Beatles. Other early favourites were T Rex and Dave Edmunds.

The white walls were slowly covered with Kate's poems and carefully coloured drawings. These were no doubt inspired by Jay's own scribblings in the grain store above the barn, where he had painted a picture he called 'The Devil's Mouth'.

While Kate submerged herself in the early psychedelic records in her brothers' collection, less than 10 miles away in Bromley another young south Londoner was about to make an onslaught on the music world. He would later call himself David Bowie. In later years Kate would often cite Bowie as a formative influence on her work.

But, up until the time she left school she really wasn't certain what she was going to do for a career. At one point psychiatry or social work were possible avenues to explore, but these thoughts, however comforting to her parents, were never really the true route for Kate to follow – and deep inside she knew this better than anyone.

Her musical confidence continued to grow, naturally encouraged by her brothers' enthusiasm for folk and English ballads; and with their mother's strong Irish background even deeper seeds for later creativity were being sown. In later years tracks like 'Night Of The Swallow', 'My Lagan Love', 'Jig Of Life' and 'The Handsome Cabin Boy' would perfectly portray the core of influences she was lucky to fall under, and she made no secret of the original inspiration. "Irish music holds so much potential for feeling and I really like it the more I get into recording the stuff. The idea of using space is interesting to me. Space and silence, because that's what makes sounds work."

Barry Plummer

The History of

East Wickham Farm

The earliest known photograph taken at East Wickham Farm shows the Wheeler family and friends on the steps to the summerhouse. This photo was taken sometime during the 1880's, prior to Mr. Gibson's occupation of the farm. **Back row, second left:** Mrs Wheeler. The chap on the far right was the house gardener.

What at one time must have been the focal point of all East Wickham, the tree lined farmhouse now stands surrounded by flats and modern suburban houses. The rear of the house has still retained a clear vantage of East Wickham open space across to Plumstead cemetery.

The farm itself has been traced back to the 1843 Tithe Apportionment, but it is thought likely that the land had been farmed long before that, which substantiates the family's 350 year old dating of the farmhouse. The shell of the house as seen today is undoubtedly much later than early 17th century and must have been built around the existing farm house, complete with its old timbers and flooring. The house has that 'added to' shape which most evolved buildings have.

In 1912 the road adjacent to the farm was made a part of Welling and East Wickham's new tramway system. No doubt the crackling of the trams passing under the overhead lines could be heard in the then solitude of East Wickham Farm.

The farmstead has remained substantially unchanged for the last 200 years. The layout of the outbuildings is more or less as recorded in the local records office of the earliest plans of the farm.

In this photograph (dated 1920), the old brick pond can be seen as the centre piece for the farm. In more recent years the Bush's have replaced the pond with a swimming pool which falls in much the same position. To the left of the picture the outbuilding was used as a granary store - the little loft above, recognisable by the opened round window, would later act as a private refuge for each of the Bush children. Kate was photographed by her brother in it in the late '60's and the round window framed her shadows in the early evening sunlight. (Unfortunately we cannot reproduce that photograph but it can be seen in John Carder Bush's 'Cathy').

Archive photos courtesy of Bexley Local Studies Dept.

Fanny on the Hill *evidently derived from the name of the original public house which stood nearby and was demolished in 1949. Local legend maintains that the pub was frequented by the notorious highwayman Dick Turpin. Even though Turpin was a brutal robber and smuggler, it is a romantic notion to picture Turpin on Black Bess sizing up nearby East Wickham Farm after a skinful in the pub!*

Mr & Mrs Bruce L Gibson, son and nurse at East Wickham Farm c.1900.

Bruce L. Gibson *was the prosperous farmer who owned and ran East Wickham farm at the turn of the century. He is seen here at the back leaning on his pitch fork with his farm workers at late harvest. Behind, in the distance is Plumstead cemetery. The view since this 1902 photograph has remained comparatively unchanged, as can be gauged by our 1988 picture. (A younger Kate with fellow schoolfriends was known to have visited the cemetery at least once for spooky Halloween thrills).*

SCHOOLDAYS

Right: *St Joseph's Convent Grammar School.*

1969

4th September 1969. Kate starts her secondary education at St. Joseph's Convent Grammar School, Abbey Wood, in South East London. In the school's end of year magazine, her first publicly written piece, a poem entitled 'Crucifixion' is published. In the same publication and listed under 'Success In Examinations', Kate is recorded as Grade 2 in violin.

St Joseph's exists today only as the name of the old wing of Erith College of Technology, the school closing in the late '70's. The front of the building, although stripped of its religious statuettes, is now listed and its attractive frontage secured. The inside of the old school hasn't been so lucky. Virtually all of the wood flooring and panelling has been removed for safety reasons and most of the rooms modernised. Rooms which have remained more or less unchanged include the art and science rooms and the gym. The school hall and stage is also as it was. The nun's quarters are now small study rooms and the whole building is criss-crossed with steep stair wells, many of them original. The only wood panelled staircase is in the reception area. (Newscaster Jan Leeming was another famous pupil of St Joseph's and in May 1988 visited the school again for a class reunion).

Kevin Cann

Omnibus Press

"I found school wasn't helping me, I became introvert. I guess it was the teachers' system, the way they react to pupils, and I wasn't quite responsive to that."

A more conventional and traditional education for Kate Bush it would be difficult to imagine.

Kate's early years were spent at St. Joseph's preparatory school in Abbey Wood, a short distance from East Wickham. Known to its pupils as 'the school on the hill' St. Joseph's accommodated around 80 mixed pupils, unlike the school opposite, St. Joseph's Grammar, which was all girls.

Kate, a shy and timid pupil, did well at prep school and passed her 11-plus. She was chosen, along with five fellow pupils, for St. Joseph's Convent Grammar School. (The following year, 1970, the 11-plus system was abolished as a nationwide system of selection.) St. Joseph's was a traditional Catholic all-girl establishment and was run by nuns who entertained a more liberal outlook, wearing modern clothes and encouraging a more free-thinking, progressive approach to schooling. This wasn't to say that the school lacked discipline, pupils were expected to work hard with a view to continuing education at university. Even though school did little for Kate's artistic aspirations, she did do well in a number of subjects including English, Latin, Biology and, of course, Music.

The school's turn-of-the-century main building was stiff and gloomy, a typical Victorian construction, complete with period desks and a labyrinth of wood-panelled corridors. Girls were reprimanded for sliding along the well polished floors and restricted from corridors which led into the nuns' quarters. Occasionally the girls would dare each other to explore forbidden territory within the school. Rumours of secret stairs and cobwebbed rooms were commonplace in earlier years and added to the mystery of the old building.

During the sixties a modern extension to the school was added, a practical and airy annexe out of keeping with the school's existing architecture. Kate's school years were spent between both buildings, studying a typical grammar school curriculum, with the school's main bias towards the sciences.

"I was unhappy at school and couldn't wait to leave," she later revealed.

"It's difficult for me to go back that far but I was quite shy. I was just a girl growing up. I learnt a few things from school which were useful, but generally it wasn't an environment I felt I could express myself in. It was just a straight school."

Whatever her inbuilt feelings towards schooling, she did manage to make the most of subjects which would later enhance her chosen career. Although music, St. Joseph's style, was of little inspirational interest, subjects like English held her concentration and found in her the qualities which would later make her both rich and famous. Although her literary flair might have led to a major novel, she moulds that skill to complement her equally skilful musical constructions. Kate's star shone in English even then, and she received her first accolades for essays and poems from teachers who realised her unusually dextrous nature, instinctively encouraging her word skills. These early invisible 'prizes', were and are, all a part of the complex puzzle in Kate's success. Kate's enthusiasm for the written word meant regular contributions to the school's end of year magazine, efforts she maintained right up until her third year, including clues to her future lyricism with a poem entitled 'Blind Joe Death'. Her first contribution, 'The Crucifixion', no doubt inspired by the hallowed surroundings of St. Joseph's, was written when she was 11.

Kate later recalled in a radio documentary: "I started writing, I suppose, when I was about 11, and it is something that has gradually progressed into what I'm doing now. I think the foundations have been laid from the minute you step out of the womb, from the environment and yourself. I used to write poetry like everyone else did in English classes and everyone was free to read them, we always read each other's work. But people at school didn't know that I was writing songs."

Like much of the content on her future LPs, Kate's earliest literary fascinations centred on isolation and being alone. "I had such an excess of emotion that I needed to get it out of my system and writing was how I did it," Kate later remembered. She used to read science fiction and was particularly keen on John Wyndham. Kate would also often recite her own stories to friends during their lunch hour. "I remember we used to sit on the black covered drains in the playground, she'd tell stories perched on the drain," a friend later recalled.

1970/71

September 1970 – June 1971. Kate in Form II at St. Joseph's Convent School. Three written pieces published in the end of year school magazine, 'A Tear And A Raindrop Met', 'Death' and 'You'.
Kate takes up piano to accompany Paddy's violin practice.

Below: *As they are today, the original art room and gym.*

Hours were also spent discussing spiritual matters, like life after death, ghosts and beliefs. In earlier years Kate and friends would act out strange stories she had created like 'The Haunted Mill' or her interpretations of Arthurian legends or the magic of Merlin. Kate's eclectic imagination was gaining apace, no doubt fuelled by the stories and thoughts of her creative brothers who encouraged her with their own discoveries.

It was around her second and third years at school that she told friends about a book she was writing, probably a children's book. No one ever saw it but the challenge of writing has remained with Kate through to today. During the early eighties Kate was known to be preparing a book entitled *Leaving My Tracks*. But it has been shelved indefinitely.

Kate was certainly no loner at school. She enjoyed the company of a select group of friends, who were welcome to visit her at home. One of her best qualities – remembered by friends – was a complete lack of sarcasm, a trait encouraged by an easy going family who didn't need such devices to score points. At a time when sarcastic wit could have been used to the full, Kate preferred to avoid all malice (although she was often picked on for no reason herself and would never retaliate).

In her fifth year at St. Joseph's Kate spent a week with friends at Newcastle Polytechnic in the halls of residence. It was at Newcastle that Kate considered a career in psychiatry, a career in which she might have excelled. "I guess it's the thinking bit, trying to communicate with people and to help them out – the emotional aspect," Kate told Harry Doherty in 1978. "It's so sad to see good, nice people screwed up when they could be so happy."

Later Kate admitted: "I didn't really want to be that. It was just to keep people happy, to think that if I did get a career it would be a straight one."

1971/72

September 1971 – June 1972. Kate's third year at St. Joseph's. She prepares two new pieces for the school magazine, 'Blind Joe Death' and 'Epitaph For A Rodent'.

Privately other poems are gradually set to music, including an early version of *The Man With The Child In His Eyes*, still a favourite of Kate's.

1972/73

September 1972 – June 1973. Fourth year at St. Joseph's.

Kate's family, with the help of music business friend Ricky Hopper, send out demo tapes in the hope of a publishing deal. The tapes were generally crammed with material and all the major record and publishing companies reject approaches.

Ricky Hopper contacts Pink Floyd's Dave Gilmour, a friend from Cambridge. Gilmour is taken with Kate's demo tapes and decides to help.

Kevin Cann

ST. JOSEPH'S CONVENT SCHOOL REVIEW

THE CRUCIFIXION

He is pushed forward from the steps,
Glistening eyes glare from around at the
dropping figure.
Silence ceases and murmurs gather quickly
like the grabbing of a hand.
Guilty onlookers hide their eyes from the
shame that they know and forbid to
reveal.
Slowly the dimness falls.
The man weeps and his forsaken tears fall
Slipping down the trembling and battered
body onto the dust.
He collapses down onto the ground.
His head bruises past the stones, scarring his
tear-stained face.
He staggers to his feet groping towards his
fate.
Sharply, iron pierces flesh, and the shape is
raised on the hill.
Stillness overcomes the cheering spectators,
And the mocked and pridebroken lead turns in outcry.
The people form and run down the hill.
He dissolves into a limp, dumb body,
As the blood red sun sinks into the skull of a dead man.
Catherine Bush (Form I)

School years were also for partying, and Kate's parties were among the best. The East Wickham farm could happily accommodate gatherings round the family's swimming pool or in the barn. Occasionally the parties would end with most of the guests jumping into the pool, to sober up a little before going home. Kate enjoyed socialising even though she was notoriously shy, but on her own turf she was in her element.

At Kate's local youth club, St. Laurence's she met her first boyfriend, Al Buckle, and shortly after her sixteenth birthday they were going steady.

Most of St. Joseph's pupils' best memories centre on the sixth form common room. The room, an attic above the old school, was in a constant state of disarray, full of old chairs and cushions. Hours were spent idly wasting lunch breaks drinking constant cups of tea or coffee, playing cards or sharing gossip. The common room was a haven of freedom and relief from the ever-increasing seriousness of exams, studying, universities and the future.

BBC

It was during Kate's Grammar school years that her musical compositions really started to take shape. Encouraged by her brothers, by her early teens she was already recording demos of her own material, some of which she would later record professionally.

Even though she was making great advances with her compositions at home, at school she made no effort to join the school orchestra, although she did sing in the school choir. Friends remembered Kate's 'above average' singing in the common room but other than that had little idea she was interested in a career in music.

All in all, Kate's school life was no different from hundreds and thousands of others up and down the country. For Kate, hours spent gazing from the window in dreams were of equal importance to the information fed to her daily via an intense school system.

"I did learn some things at school," Kate would later say, but perhaps the best lesson of all was that the music she carried in her head made the drudgery of school more bearable.

"One day I was with a friend in a park and just knew that (music) was what I wanted to do. I had to leave school and I had to do it then and I'm very glad I did," Kate later recalled in a TV interview.

Kate eventually left St. Joseph's in 1975 with 10 'O' levels and high hopes of a publishing deal for songs her family knew were of real quality. Although Kate's mother and father were naturally apprehensive of her sudden decision to take on the world of music, they accepted and supported her wishes. Kate was no fool with unattainable hopes but more of a practical dreamer with goals of writing and recording her own material. Her decision to pursue music professionally lifted years of indecision from her shoulders, but even the talented Catherine Bush couldn't have forseen that her talent would take her to the top, in real style, quite so suddenly.

Above: *Kate at home in the vast fireplace of East Wickham Farm.*

Far Left: *Little of the original wood panelling survives, the religious statuettes have gone, but St Joseph's facade is now listed.*

Below: *Did Kate play on these old school pianos?*

Kevin Cann

15

EMI AND THE KICK INSIDE

Barry Plummer

1973/74

September 1973 – June 1974. Fifth year of secondary school.

Kate records two songs, *Passing Through The Air* and *Maybe* with Dave Gilmour at his home studio. The new and improved demos are still turned down by record companies.

1974/75

September 1974 – June 1975. Kate stays on into her sixth year at school but leaves during the summer holidays of 1975, returning to the school only once after that for a brief visit. She leaves with 10 'O' levels and an ever-increasing interest in music and dance, but at this stage is still unclear exactly how to express those feelings.

"When I was at school poetry was my thing, then I got into songs – it was much more exciting."(KB 1978)

From as early as 12 or 13 Kate had recorded her songs on her brother's tape recorder and gradually built up a vast compilation of 60 or more on several cassettes. Ricky Hopper, a friend of the family, was in the music business and he helped her send these demo tapes to all the main publishers and record companies but there was no response.

Ricky played a cassette to his Cambridge friend Dave Gilmour, singer and guitarist with Pink Floyd, and invited him to come and hear the young prodigy. Kate had never met this rock star of course but he was no stranger to her thoughts. Her schoolfriend Diane Carman recalled a couple of years before: "The first boy she ever had a crush on, she used to call him Gilmour. We used to walk for hours hoping to catch a glimpse in the freezing cold. I think she only spoke to him once and that was about it." Now the original came to the farmhouse and met a very nervous girl of 14 who played and sang him some of her songs.

It is fair to assume that Dave was as taken with Kate as she was with him. She could hardly have found a more helpful patron. He was immediately impressed and in due course took her to his own home studio, a modest 16-track, at his farm near Harlow in Essex. They recorded a number of songs, including 'Maybe' and 'Passing Through Air' (this song became the B-side of 'Army Dreamers' in 1980) and sent these demos round again but still they were turned down.

So in June Dave Gilmour introduced Kate to EMI record producer Andrew Powell at the Pink Floyd office and together they sifted through three or four cassettes of over 60 songs to choose three for a professional demo.

With Dave Gilmour footing the bill and Andrew producing, Kate recorded the songs at AIR studios in central London in a suite of offices high above Oxford Circus – 'The Man With The Child In His Eyes', 'Saxophone Song' and 'Maybe'. These were fully professional studios and the results were so good that two of the tracks were later included on 'The Kick Inside' – though Kate didn't know it then she had just recorded her second single and started work on her first album! ('Maybe' has never appeared however.) Dave Gilmour was away on tour at the time – he is simply credited as Executive Producer.

It was now the summer holidays of 1975 and Kate was looking beyond the suburban confines of Welling and East Wickham. The last two years at school had been hopeful but seemed to have led nowhere. In July Kate had her seventeenth birthday and made an important decision – school had no more to offer and it was time to leave. With 10 'O' Levels behind her she knew that her real interest was music, though at this stage she had no clear idea of what her career might be.

Dave Gilmour also made a decision. Kate's latest demo tape was excellent and he had no intention of letting it fall on the stony ground of A&R men's desks. This time he would go straight to the top. Pink Floyd were recording 'Wish You Were Here' at EMI's Abbey Road studios and this gave him the opportunity he needed. One day EMI pop division general manager Bob Mercer came by to see how The Floyd were doing and Dave asked him to listen to the new demo tape. Bob was very impressed, particularly by her precocious writing talent – he could hardly believe she had been writing these songs since her early teens. "The singer's vocal peculiarity, her range so wide and strong really appealed to me," he said. When he met her he realised she had the potential to be a star. "A gamine quality that suggests sexual innocence." Bob's colleague Terry Slater, who had signed The Sex Pistols, phoned Kate and invited her to EMI for an interview. "She was overwhelmed that somebody would be interested in what she was doing." But Terry was very interested and "realised she was somebody special."

Kate was now directly in touch with the powers-that-be in the world's largest record company, but events still moved slowly and it wasn't until the following summer that a deal was signed. In those early days EMI didn't know quite how to market her and felt that she needed to develop. "On meeting her I realised how young she was mentally," Bob expained. Dave Gilmour couldn't really help any further – he had commitments with his own band and he never made a move to manage her. But Kate was well aware of how much Dave had done for her. "He was looking around for unknown talent. He came along and heard me and we put some things down, and he put up the money for me to make my first demo in a proper recording studio with arrangements. I owe it all to him, that I got my contract and where I am now."

Meanwhile Kate was in limbo. She had left school but found no immediate career. EMI were still considering her but had offered nothing concrete. Then quite by chance something happened which opened Kate's eyes to a whole new world and suggested a wider scope for her talents. A single performance by Lindsay Kemp, the outrageous master of mime, was enough to shake off her depression.

1975

June 1975. Dave Gilmour pays for Kate to record at London's AIR studios. Kate meets Andrew Powell for the first time. Powell and Gilmour sift through over 60 tracks from Kate's demos to choose three songs to record: *The Man With The Child In His Eyes, Saxophone Song* and *Maybe*. Two of these tracks would eventually make Kate's first LP release.

July 1975. Kate takes her mock 'A' level exams at St. Joseph's.
Around this time Dave Gilmour encourages EMI pop division general manager Bob Mercer to listen to Kate's new demo tape. The recordings impress Mercer. EMI start negotiations. The deal is carefully prepared but not signed until 1976.

Summer 1975. Kate attends classes run by the famous mime artist Lindsay Kemp at the Dance Centre, Floral Street, Covent Garden. Kate is enthused after attending a performance of Genet's *Flowers* by Kemp at the Collegiate Theatre, London.
The courses stretched Kate's resources (at this point an inheritance left to her by an aunt), but she was now feeling happier and starting to realise something of a growing ambition.

Barry Plummer

Left: *Kate at EMI.*

Kate went to see Kemp's solo show *Flowers* and was electrified. She realised, as had David Bowie before her, that here was a way to project herself and her music. She started attending classes by Kemp and others. From now on her life would revolve around London's dance studios as she absorbed all she could of these new talents and disciplines.

Kate had lived most of her life on the edge of London in the small sheltered area of Kent between her home and school but now she was to take the plunge into London's glamour and sleaze at the edges of the world of entertainment. Though at first shy, she took to her new life like a duck to water. When Lindsay's classes finished she attended various courses at the Dance Centre in Floral Street, Covent Garden, learning contemporary dance, a few ballet hints and anything else which caught her imagination. One of her teachers was Arlene Phillips who created the dance group Hot Gossip.

A chance find at this time would come to fruition years later. "When I used to go up to the Dance Centre in London I went into Watkins occult bookshop for a look and there was this book, 'A Book Of Dreams' by Peter Reich. I just thought it was going 'Hello, hello,' so I picked the book up and couldn't believe that I'd just *found* this book on a shelf. It was so inspirational, very magical." The book formed the basis for 'Cloudbusting' eight years later.

Around this time Kate moved out from the family farmhouse into her own flat, but she was still very much under the family wing. This was at the top of a house in Lewisham and below were her two brothers, Paddy in a flat full of guitars and other instruments, and Jay with his family on the ground floor.

1976

(Early) 1976. Kate attends mime classes run by Adam Durius in an arts complex in Elephant and Castle, South London.

March 1976. Kate takes her driving test for the first time but fails.

July 1976. Kate signs to EMI records after nearly a year of negotiations. She is given a £3,000 advance and is allowed the space to widen and improve before any material is publicly released.

30th July 1976. Kate's eighteenth birthday.

August 1976. Re–takes her driving test and passes.

In July 1976 Kate finally signed to EMI after meetings involving Dave Gilmour and her family. But even now the company felt she was not ready to plunge in as a recording artist. Andrew Powell believes they were still uncertain how to present her – she hardly fitted into any of the normal pop categories. So they agreed to pay her an advance of £3000 (plus £500 from EMI Publishing for her songs) while she continued writing and grooming herself. "We gave her some money to grow up with," as Bob Mercer put it.

During the following year Kate demoed further songs and had to resist pressure from EMI to make them more commercial before releasing anything. ("Not so heavy – more hook lines.") These months were difficult and frustrating but she kept her head and continued the process of development from a precocious schoolgirl to an artist whom EMI could confidently launch on an unsuspecting world.

But something was going to happen. Saturday March 5 1977 was a full moon and that night Kate was inspired to write a strange, untamed song about Cathy, the doomed heroine of Emily Brontë's only novel. "I'm sure one of the reasons it stuck in my mind was because of the spirit of Cathy. As a child I was called Cathy. It was just a matter of exaggerating all my bad areas because she's a really vile person. She's just so headstrong and passionate and crazy, you know. It was fun to do – it took a night and a half!"

In April her brother Paddy put together a band called the KT Bush Band and they played pub gigs in London throughout that summer until July. Then EMI finally invited her back into AIR Studios to start work seriously on her first album and songs from

which her first single would be chosen. This was Kate's best birthday present! She was now 19.

Andrew Powell was to produce the album – he had arranged the successful three-track demo for Dave Gilmour and again they scrutinised the cassettes of songs to select a mere dozen for the album. "'The Kick Inside' is not something that just suddenly happened," explains Kate. "It's years of work, because since I was a kid I've always been writing songs and it was really just collecting together all the best songs that I had and putting them on the album. Really years of preparation and inspiration that got it together."

The musicians for the session were mostly from a couple of in-house EMI bands – from Cockney Rebel came Stuart Elliot on drums and Duncan MacKay on keyboards and guitar, and from Pilot came Andrew's friend Ian Bairnson on guitar and David Paton on bass. At this stage Andrew and EMI were not prepared to take chances on untried musicians in the studio so Paddy only played on one track, and other members of the KT Bush Band were completely excluded. (Kate later brought them back into the fold for the tour, and after that they joined her in the studio for subsequent albums.) Andrew himself played on several of the tracks as producers often do – bass, various keyboards and even beer bottles!

Ever since the advent of multi-track tape recording in the sixties it has become the usual practice to record rock music with the backing first and then let the vocalist add the lead line after the basic instruments have been recorded to everyone's satisfaction. But because of the way she wrote the songs Kate preferred to sit down at the piano and play and sing with the band right from the start. This made for a tremendous 'live' feel and although she might re-do her vocal later this fresh spark of performance remained. And it was extraordinary how polished her original 'guide' vocal would be.

1977

March 1977. Kate writes *Wuthering Heights* which would, in less than a year, be her first single release and her first number one.

Below: *Lindsay Kemp performing 'Flowers' at the Collegiate Theatre in 1975. "He had such an incredible aura. He taught me that you can express with your body — and when your body is awake so is your mind." K.B.*

BBC

BBC

19

1977

April 1977. The KT Bush Band formed by Paddy and Kate. Paddy enrols friends Brian Bath, Charlie Morgan and Del Palmer.

The band's opening gig was a tough Lewisham venue, the Rose of Lee pub, where they went on to perform at least five more times. Material included *Brown Sugar, Satisfaction* and her own *James And The Cold Gun*. The band toured around London until June/July when Kate had to leave to prepare for recording her first album.

The KT Bush Band were filmed backing Kate for her first TV appearance on West German TV in 1978.

July/August 1977. After two years of frustration, Kate is invited into the recording studio to start work on her first LP. Andrew Powell, who had arranged the successful three–track demo for Dave Gilmour, was now producer. Session musicians included various members of Cockney Rebel and Pilot – EMI stable mates.

September 1977. *Wuthering Heights* is chosen as the first single release, Kate's choice over EMI's *James And The Cold Gun.*

4th November 1977. *Wuthering Heights* single, planned for release on this date, delayed because of Kate's insistence to change sleeve design. The delay sets the release date back until the new year, even though Capital Radio create much interest in Kate by playing an advance pressing of the single two months before it is actually released.

They generally started early in the afternoon – mornings are not popular with musicians! So that first day Kate sat down at the piano and played and sang 'Moving', 'L'Amour Looks Something Like You' and 'Wuthering Heights'. Jon Kelly was the engineer at that session and he was immediately impressed by Kate and her songs. "She had a star quality about her that you couldn't ignore."

At first she was still pretty green about what could and should be done but she learned fast. Jon Kelly engineered on the first two albums and then helped Kate produce the third. He remembered that she was very interested in everything that happened in the studio and wanted to know more and more about it – how things were recorded and how to change and develop sounds to make them more interesting.

The whole album was finished in seven weeks, short even for a first album. The first single would be chosen from among these tracks and the album was ready for release if the single was a hit.

The first sound on the album is the mournful keening of whales – which to Kate is the sound of a friendly world which we should be able to embrace. She was very keen on whales when she was younger and tried to write a whale song. The cover shows Kate hanging on a kite floating past an enormous all-seeing eye.

'Moving' is a strange but beautiful song in which (as in many songs) she seems to be clasping a lover to her with one arm while pushing him away with the other. The second word is 'stranger' but she may be singing to a lover who feels like a stranger. Or she may, as in 'The Man With The Child In His Eyes', be imagining a lover. Then she asks, 'Does it really matter as long as you're not afraid to feel' – this desire/fear to surrender to love is a constant theme (most intensely expressed later in 'Hounds Of Love').

In the chorus she sings, 'You give me life – please don't let me go!' – it could be a line straight out of 'Wuthering Heights'. Kate displays a constant fear of being cut off from people, from the world, from life. This sense of alienation haunts many of her songs – in 'The Saxophone Song' it's hard to decide whether she's talking to a person she knows intimately or just someone she has seen and is fantasizing about. 'All the people in the club are babbling but the instrument is talking, and I can but listen.' This was one of the songs recorded in that demo session back in 1975 when she was 17.

'Strange Phenomena' is the first of her 'philosophical' songs in which she struggles to make sense of the world and her place in it. This search continues ('Symphony In Blue', 'Blow Away', and 'Sat In Your Lap') until the philosophy becomes a part of her. After 'Never For Ever' the questions about life are implicit in her writing – the personal-philosophical like the personal-political.

LFI

20th January 1978. *Wuthering Heights/ Kite* single released. Kate performs the single live for delegates of the EMI international sales conference.

Kate appears live on Tony Myatt's *Late Show* on Capital Radio for her first radio interview.

Here she seems to throw superstitions together quite casually – while showing a strong desire to make sense of a world which has more to it than meets the eye. The moon controls a tide in the affairs of woman. "It's all about coincidences – similar things seem to attract together like the saying, 'Birds of a feather flock together'."

"There's a school of thought about that called Synchronicity. It's about how one day all these really strange coincidences will happen to you. I think by what you think and how you are you attract things to you. If you're a negative unhappy person I really believe a lot of negative unhappy things could happen to you."

There is more to life than meets the eye and in 'Kite' she cries out that she wants to feel it – though it frightens her when she lets herself go. 'Beelzebub is aching in my belly' – maybe this is one of the demons that later bursts out of her on 'Never For Ever', or the first stirring of a kick inside. There is strong sexual imagery here, as with flying.

In John (Jay) Bush's recent book of photos *Cathy* there is a charming picture of her as a child in a huge pair of adult riding boots. But 'rooted in my wellios' may be a cry against suburban Welling – 'and I want to get away!'

'The Man With The Child In His Eyes' is a classic ballad and yet so different from an ordinary love song. The inspiration for this song "was just a particular thing that happened when I went to the piano. The piano just started speaking to me." It is probably the earliest song to survive into her recorded work – she wrote a version of it on the wall of her den when she was 14, a young girl's fantasy lover. "This was about an adult who is still very much of a child and could still take a delight in the innocence of things. In some men I think it's a positive thing to sometimes not let go of that. I liked the idea of the innocence of a person shining in their eyes. How wonderful it is that they manage to retain this magic."

Kate was – and still is – very proud of this song and later insisted it should be the second single rather than 'Them Heavy People'. She wanted to prove that she didn't only write freaky songs like 'Wuthering Heights' and that she could sing a simple song in an unaffected voice.

'Wuthering Heights' has Kate telling a story for the first time – using another character to explore herself. Cathy – the ghost and the songwriter – is afraid of leaving home. She is insubstantial and cut off from real people – this sense of depersonalisation occurs again and again in Kate's songs.

'James And The Cold Gun' is a jaunty rock song about a cowboy (Jesse James?). This is the nearest Kate ever came to mainstream pop – with raunchy Elton John-style piano. It touches on themes to which she will keep returning. James today could be a soldier, a freedom-fighter or a terrorist ('Night Of The Swallow').

On this side of the album we get 'home', 'parlour', 'floor', 'boudoir', 'a room in my mind', 'lace and chintz' and 'room for the life'. Kate identifies herself very strongly with home – the farmhouse in which she grew up with its overgrown garden and wooden fence. A room is reassuring and protective but it can also become a claustrophobic cage from which she needs to break free.

BBC

1978

21st January 1978. First press reviews appear. Although many papers decide to ignore the record completely, Rosalind Russell commented in *Record Mirror* that it was a "rotten song", but concluded that it could be a hit on its novelty value.

7th February 1978. *Wuthering Heights* enters the BMRB charts at number 42. The following week (February 14th) it had made number 27.

9th February 1978. Kate travels by plane for the first time to promote *Wuthering Heights* in Germany and Holland. Makes her first TV appearance with the KT Bush Band on top magazine programme *Bio's Bahnhof* in West Germany, a deliberate low–key broadcast to build confidence for possible UK TV work. The show was filmed in the usual disused tram station which is the programme's setting. Kate and band performed *Kite* and *Wuthering Heights*.

While Kate was in Europe, *Wuthering Heights* had entered the top 50.

16th February 1978. Kate makes her first appearance on *Top Of The Pops* in a sheer black top, red slacks and black stiletto heels. The energetic performance did not impress her when she watched the playback.

By this time not only the music press but also the nationals had picked up on the unusual qualities of Kate Bush, and she was interviewed by virtually every music magazine and newspaper going. These interviews started to appear towards the end of February.

During the rest of the month, Kate made further TV appearances on ITV's *Magpie* children's show, the BBC's *Saturday Night At The Mill* (performing live *Them Heavy People* and *Moving*) – (February 25th).

Above Right: *Kate photographed by Gered Mankowitz for the US cover of 'The Kick Inside'.*

'Feel It', sung alone at the piano, is charming for its sensuality and frankness. Kate adopts what might be a 'little girl drunk' voice. It is interesting how she uses the word 'parlour' – which could be a friendly family room or the lair of a spider.

'Feel It' and the two songs which follow may be about one-night-stands but as with 'Moving' this is not made clear. A lover may always remain a stranger to some degree. In 'Oh To Be In Love' the music seems at odds with the words but it may be Kate's sense of humour slipping in or even more nervous laughter. 'L'Amour Looks Something Like You' is Kate at her most charming though even in such a romantic mood she is not afraid to remember 'sticky love inside' – also a good image for an uncomfortable emotion.

'Them Heavy People' celebrates Kate's discovery of philosophy. Her brothers introduced her to many ancient and exotic ideas including those of G.I. Gurdjieff, an Armenian mystic and philosopher. Maybe she has joined the 'heavy people' herself – if they rolled the ball to her she certainly picked it up. But she feels this is something anyone can do – 'we humans got it all.' Yes, if we can only find it!

All through this side of the album there are images of rooms and on the last two songs Kate's thoughts focus deep inside as she makes the identification of a room with the womb. Woman is the first home of every human life and this gives her a strength which she does not have to prove. ('Room For The Life').

"'The Kick Inside', which is the title track, was inspired by a traditional folk song and it was an area that I wanted to explore because it's one that is really untouched, and that is one of incest. There are so many songs about love but they're always on such an obvious level. This song is about a brother and a sister who are in love and the sister becomes pregnant by her brother. Because it is so taboo and unheard of, she kills herself in order to protect her brother's name and the family. The song is a suicide note, and it's the sister saying, 'Right, I'm doing it for you so don't worry and I'll come back someday'."

As in many of her songs Kate is using someone else's situation to explore her own. Here she is in the home pulling down her lace and the chintz. There are many overtones – smoothing down petticoats to hide herself but tearing down the curtains to let light into the house. She is changing the home, altering her relationship to her family – to her brothers. The song speaks in terms of incest but in Kate's case it is more about growing up and growing away.

Kate used the two years EMI had given her to develop to the full, but she often felt impatient waiting for the time when she would be called to record her first LP.

The situation improved, however, when Paddy and Kate got together to form a new band. They called it The KT Bush Band and it provided the backbone to most of Kate's future recording and live performance.

Among the original line up at rehearsal stage was a drummer called Vic King, soon to be replaced by Charlie Morgan, who settled the line-up along with Brian Bath on guitar, Del Palmer on bass, Paddy on rhythm and acoustic guitar and Kate as lead vocalist. The early magic worked and has remained for her to draw upon ever since (even though Paddy was the only KTBB member to make an appearance on her first LP, recorded shortly after the band's formation).

Kate made a big impression on her new band members, especially Del Palmer: "I'd heard about Kate from Paddy 'cos I'd known him for some time. I felt a particular emotional involvement coming on right from the word go. I knew I had to get involved in some way because this was going to be MEGA. lt was a phenomenon because it was so different to what anyone else was doing."

The band's first engagement was at The Rose of Lee pub in Lewisham, not in the most salubrious of districts. This first public performance was a hard gig at which she performed well and confidently. Naturally before the first show she was very nervous, but she soon overcame this as the performance itself took priority for her concentration. With EMI ready to push her into every corner of the musical globe this was just as well.

All of the audiences were very enthusiastic towards the band, even a large bunch of rowdy Scottish football supporters enjoyed the show during a gig in Putney – some even took to the stage with Kate, trying to sing along with her, waving their flags before the following day's England-Scotland game.

Most of the KT Bush Band's repertoire consisted of the usual pub band covers. Songs like 'Brown Sugar', 'I Heard It Through The Grapevine', 'Sweet Soul Music', 'Honky Tonk Woman' and The Beatles' 'Come Together'. They did, however, perform a few of Kate's tracks like 'James And The Cold Gun', which went down equally well.

The band was also notable for bringing Kate and Del Palmer together. Their relationship has continued to flourish over the years and Del has become an important collaborator during the whole of Kate's creative process; acting as engineer during the original demos, musician, sound mixer and occasional art advisor (sleeve design for 'The Kick Inside'). Kate has since said she needed to take time off to "fall in love."

The KT Bush Band was always to be a short-lived vehicle, soon it would be Kate alone who would take centre stage. The band had been an invaluable encouragement for Kate and she gained valuable confidence in the months leading up to the recording of her first LP.

"They were frustrating times," Kate later commented. "But it was worth waiting for. I had so much more confidence and experience when I finally got started."

1978

17th February 1978. Kate's début LP *The Kick Inside* released.

THE KICK INSIDE (EMI) EMC 3223

Side One
Moving
drums: Stuart Elliot
bass: David Paton
guitars: Ian Bairnson
electric piano: Duncan Mackay

The Saxophone Song
drums: Barry de Souza
bass: Bruce Lynch
guitars: Paul Keogh, Alan Parker
keyboards: Andrew Powell
saxophone: Alan Skidmore
electric guitar: Paul Keogh

Strange Phenomena
drums: Stuart Elliot
bass: David Paton
guitars: Ian Bairnson
electric piano: Andrew Powell
synthesizer: Duncan Mackay
percussion: Morris Pert

Kite
drums: Stuart Elliot
bass: David Paton
guitars: Ian Bairnson
organ/clavinet: Duncan Mackay
percussion: Morris Pert

The Man With The Child In His Eyes

Wuthering Heights
drums: Stuart Elliot
bass: Andrew Powell
acoustic guitars: David Paton
electric guitar: Ian Bairnson
organ: Duncan Mackay
celeste: Andrew Powell
percussion: Morris Pert

BBC

23

WUTHERING HEIGHTS

1978

Side Two
James And The Cold Gun
drums: Stuart Elliot
bass: David Paton
guitars: Ian Bairnson
organ: Duncan Mackay

Feel It

Oh To Be In Love
drums: Stuart Elliot
bass: David Paton
guitars: David Paton, Ian Bairnson
mandolin: Paddy Bush
synthesizer: Andrew Powell
percussion: Stuart Elliot
backing vocals: David Paton, Ian Bairnson

L'Amour Looks Something Like You
drums: Stuart Elliot
bass: David Paton
guitars: Ian Bairnson
electric piano: Duncan Mackay

Them Heavy People
drums: Stuart Elliot
bass: David Paton
guitars: Ian Bairnson
backing vocals: Paddy and Kate Bush

Room For The Life
drums: Stuart Elliot
bass: David Paton
guitars: Ian Bairnson,
Boo–Bams(!), Morris Pert
percussion: Stuart Elliot
beer bottles: Andrew Powell,
Ian Bairnson

Above Right: *Part of Kate's routine for the 'Wuthering Heights' video.*

Gered Mankowitz

"Cathy will live on as a force, I was lucky she stopped in me long enough to write a song."

It was a cold February, 1978, and 'Wuthering Heights' arrived over the air waves like an unidentified flying object. No one could believe what they were hearing – they had no idea where it was coming from. It was one of those records – those events – that everyone could remember the first time they heard it:
"I was doing the washing up, not really listening to the radio when . . ."
"I was driving down the M4 listening out for a snow forecast when . . ."
"This bloke upstairs had the radio on really loud . . ."
"Have you heard that ridiculous record . . .?"
Love it or hate it, everyone had a reaction. Kate Bush did not inspire indifference.

It was not the record company's first choice. EMI wanted 'James And The Cold Gun' but Kate's decision prevailed and in September 'Wuthering Heights' was scheduled as the first single. This was an extraordinary victory for a new and untried artist but she was very determined and Pink Floyd still carried a considerable weight of patronage. When asked on a phone-in (February 1979) how much say she had in what was released, she said, "Quite a lot – probably more than I'm entitled to. But we discuss it – it's not really saying 'I want this' and them going 'We want this'. We do come to a compromise and a discussion – it's quite human!"

She won a further battle over the sleeve design. EMI wanted the picture of her in a pink cotton vest, eyes wide, lips parted and her nipples clearly outlined. She vetoed this single-sleeve but the picture became a major part of EMI's promotion campaign, splashed all over London on buses and hoardings, mesmerising the city's commuters. "I suppose the poster is reasonably sexy just 'cos you can see my tits, but I think the vibe from my face is there. Often you get pictures of females showing their legs with a very plastic face. I think that poster projects a mood."

Gered Mankowitz, who took this picture, has always specialised in pop people. He was The Rolling Stones' official photographer in the sixties. "When I first heard 'Wuthering Heights', I knew that if it got *any* airplay, people would want to hear it again – and that's exactly how I approached the first photo session . . . that if people saw her once, they'd want to see her again. I photographed her a lot after this, but I don't think I ever quite re-captured the magic of the first picture. It's really simple and it really works."

These changes delayed the release date – November 1977 – and rather than chance the single sinking in the Christmas flood of new records it was decided to wait until the new year.

However several promotional copies had been sent out to radio stations and at London's Capital Radio producer Eddie Puma picked it out for Tony Myatt's *Late Show*.

"We did try to keep in the forefront of new product and it was incredibly striking." So Tony played the song two months before release though he and Eddie had a hard time convincing anyone it would be a hit. Everyone thought it was really weird.

"My first reaction was, 'My God, I've never heard anything like this!' Then people started calling up and saying, 'What's that unbelievable record?'."

On January 20 1978 'Wuthering Heights' was at last officially released. Kate performed the song live for delegates at an EMI sales conference and did her first interview on Tony Myatt's *Late Show*. He was just as taken with her in person. "She was 19 years old, and looked so young and so pretty, and when we started talking she was so intelligent. She was easy to talk to and unaffected by it all – so much beauty and talent was unbelievable in one person. After our interview everything started to snowball for her – everyone wanted to talk to Kate Bush."

Gered Mankowitz

Left: *From the controversial Gered Mankowitz photo session.*

1978

The Kick Inside
Produced and arranged by Andrew Powell
Engineer: Jon Kelly
Recorded at AIR London Studios: July/August 1977
Executive producer on **The Man With The Child In His Eyes** and **The Saxophone Song**: Dave Gilmour – June 1975.
Backing and lead vocals: Kate Bush
Piano: Kate Bush
Orchestral contractor: David Katz
All songs written by: Kate Bush
Sleeve concept: Kate Bush
Front cover design: Splash Design
Photography: Jay Myrdal
Back cover original ideas: John Carder Bush and Del Palmer
Kate's sleeve notes were neat and precise: "Much thanks and love to Dave Gilmour for 'rolling the ball' in the beginning, the KT Bush Band for giving it a kick, EMI for 'the strange phenomena', my teachers of music and movement for being 'heavy' and to all of you with open ears – please feel it."

21st February 1978. *Wuthering Heights* continues to climb the charts, making number 13 (number five on February 28th).

7th March 1978. *Wuthering Heights* makes number one. Having already gone silver, it was only a short wait before it also picked up a gold award. Kate celebrates at a champagne reception in Paris and later buys a £7,000 Steinway piano for her East Wickham Farm rehearsal room.

8th March 1978. *The Daily Express* wrote "Wuthering Wonderful", the paper spouting that newcomer Kate Bush had dislodged Abba from the top slot.

The Daily Mirror wrote "A tonic for the doctor's daughter!" Kate Bush had suddenly become hot property and offers for interviews poured in; she even made an appearance on current affairs programme *Today*. Kate Bush, it would seem, had arrived . . .

16th March 1978. Kate is interviewed on BBC2's *Tonight* programme.

25th March 1978. Kate visits Ireland on a four–day promotional trip. Appears on the *Late Late Show*.

1978

March 1978 (Late). *The Kick Inside* LP released in the US. (Capitol.)

April 1978 (Early). *Wuthering Heights* starts to slide down the charts after four weeks at number one.

The Kick Inside peaks in the UK album charts at number three by mid–April.

Wuthering Heights had not only made number one in the UK, but most countries in western Europe, where it had either made the top slot or the top three. But America seemed more reluctant to fall, despite a quick promotional visit from Kate. (Arrives back in the UK 21st April.)

16th May 1978. Kate performs dramatised versions of seven of her songs from *The Kick Inside* for a Dutch TV programme. Filmed at De Efteling gardens near Amsterdam.

20th May 1978. Performs *Them Heavy People* on Mickie Most's pilot ATV programme, *Revolver*. Peter Cook introduces her as "Basil Brush's younger sister," who had the great hit "Withering Tights". (Programme recorded in March 1978.)

26th May 1978. The follow-up single to *Wuthering Heights* was expected to be *Them Heavy People*, but this was changed on Kate's insistence to a song she had written and originally demoed with Dave Gilmour in 1975 when she was 17, *The Man With The Child In His Eyes*. The music and lyrics actually went back to her early teens and was one of the first songs she had set to music. The song had actually formed part of the demo which had secured her EMI contract. The original lyrics had been penned on to the wall of Kate's personal 'secret' room in her house, a song which was, and still is, very close to her.

On the 19th May, the song had been previewed to the BBC Radio One panel of Kid Jensen, Peter Powell and Manfred Mann who all gave it the thumbs up. Even the music press couldn't afford to ignore the new Kate Bush single.

Right: *Kate and Heathcliff arriving at Heathrow.*

The following day the first press reviews appeared. Many papers decided to ignore the record but Rosalind Russell in *Record Mirror* thought it was a "rotten song" but could be a hit on its novelty value. Ian Birch in *Melody Maker* was the most articulate:

"Bizarre. Kate is a complete newcomer, is 19, was first unearthed by Dave Gilmour, and has spent time with mime coach to the stars, Lindsay Kemp . . . The theatre influence comes through strongly from the cover . . . to every aspect of Kate's song. The orchestration is ornate and densely packed, but never overflows its banks, Kate's extraordinary vocals skating in and out, over and above.

"Reference points are tricky, but possibly a cross between Linda Lewis and Macbeth's three witches is the closest. She turns the famous examination text by Emily Brontë into glorious soap opera trauma . . . "

Two weeks later 'Wuthering Heights' entered the BMRB charts at number 42 – whatever their initial reaction people were now buying it.

Kate travelled to Germany and Holland with the KT Bush Band to promote the single. She made her first TV appearance on top rating West German magazine programme *Bio's Bahnhof* miming in the disused tram station that is the show's setting. She also performed 'Kite' (the B-side) live with the band. The trip was her first flight and she loved the experience, unlike many pop people. "It was mind-blowing – I *really* want to do more of that!"

In the following weeks the single leapt to number 27, then 13, then into the Top 10 at number five. Kate made her first appearance on *Top Of The Pops* in a black top, red slacks and black stiletto heels. When she saw this performance later she said, "It was like watching myself die – a bloody awful performance." Maybe that was when she decided she would master the art of performance, television and video. It may also be one reason why she took so long preparing for her tour – everything had to be right.

Something Kate soon decided was not right was her management. At first her family had naturally taken an interest and involved themselves in the early negotiations with EMI. In due course Jay had fallen into the unofficial capacity of manager, with Paddy

keeping an eye on the music side. Once Kate started to record and business began in earnest, EMI executives found that management by family committee created problems. Terry Walker suggested his friend Peter Lyster-Todd, who had worked in theatre production and even managed Lord Snowdon. At first he got on well with the family but during the early months of success they came to resent his involvement. There was a brief exchange of solicitors' letters but, as Lyster-Todd commented, "Eventually we got everything sorted out amicably."

A more diplomatic set-up was then arranged with Hilary Walker, Terry's ex-wife who had worked for Bob Mercer. 'Hil' had a more sensitive touch than Lyster-Todd and was described as Kate's assistant, really an executive manager. In due course Jay resumed the official title. In the long run this 'unprofessional' arrangement has worked well and Kate is one of the few successful pop artists to avoid a costly and public management dispute at some point in her career.

On March 7 'Wuthering Heights' made number one. It had already gone silver and soon after picked up a gold award for half a million sales in Britain. Kate celebrated at a champagne reception in Paris and later bought a £7,000 Steinway piano for her East Wickham rehearsal room. With Paddy's help she had turned an old barn there into a dance/demo-studio with an 8-track recorder, financing the project from her EMI advance. Over the years she would develop this studio until it became a fully equipped commercial recording studio.

Throughout the month Kate was the subject of articles and interviews in the national press and even appeared on current affairs programmes – *Today* on ITV and *Tonight* on BBC2. In two short months Kate Bush had arrived!

"It was an incredible surprise. You know, you think, 'Well I'd like it to get in the charts,' and it gets in the charts and you think, 'Great, it's in the charts.' And next week it's still in the charts and it's going up. The last thing I thought was, 'No, it will never do it . . .' top five! And each time you think, 'My God, it's just not going to do it.' In fact the morning it got there someone I hadn't met for a couple of years rang me up and said, 'Congratulations!' and I didn't understand what he was talking about and he said, 'Oh you're number one,' and I just went, 'Wow'!"

Wuthering Heights is a romantic nineteenth century novel by Emily Brontë, one of three Victorian sisters from the Yorkshire village of Haworth, all of whom wrote. Emily wrote mostly poetry concerned with an imaginary land, and *Wuthering Heights* was her only novel. It took her seven years to write and was only published after her death. Kate has taken considerable interest in Emily Brontë and discovered the eerie fact that they were both born on July 30! Some of Emily's passionate poetry is surprisingly similar in mood to some of Kate's lines:

> 'No coward soul is mine,
> No trembler in the world's storm-troubled sphere:
> I see Heaven's glories shine,
> And faith shines equal, arming me from fear.'
> (*Last Lines*)

The story is set on the Yorkshire Moors – "Wuthering being a significant provincial adjective, descriptive of the atmospheric tumult". It could as well describe the emotions which keep the passionate heroine Catherine Earnshaw and the wild and wilful Heathcliff apart until death, when they are buried side by side.

Kate had seen the classic film (1938) on television with Merle Oberon as Cathy and Laurence Olivier as the brooding Heathcliff. "It's about the end of the film where Cathy has died and she's coming back as a spirit across the moors to get Heathcliff again. It struck me very strongly that it shows a lot about human beings because if they can't get what they want they will go to such extremes in order to do it. And this is what she did – she didn't even leave him alone when she was dead, she had to come back and get him, and I found it amazing."

The film so caught Kate's imagination that she read the book, and felt the spirit of the book was captured in the final page. The narrator is walking home by a full moon and stops by the ruined church to look at the three headstones – the middle one (Catherine's) grey and half buried in heath; her husband's "only harmonised by the turf, and moss creeping up its foot; Heathcliff's still bare.

"I lingered round them, under that benign sky: watched the moths fluttering among the heath and hare-bells; listened to the soft wind breathing through the grass; and wondered how any one could ever imagine unquiet slumbers for the sleepers in that quiet earth.

"I felt I just had to write a song about the tormented heroine Cathy calling for the soul of Heathcliff so they could be together eternally. It was a real challenge to précis the whole mood of a book into such a short piece."

In April as the single started its inevitable slide the LP 'The Kick Inside' reached its peak position at number three in the UK charts. It was released the day after Kate's first *Top Of The Pops* appearance and in due course went double platinum. Its sales were only surpassed by 'The Whole Story' compilation in 1987. The single had also made the top three in most European countries. But America felt – and still feels – that this unique voice was just too weird.

1978

3rd June 1978. *Record Mirror*: "It can't fail. She alternates between a little–girl voice and mental seduction . . . buy it – preferably one for every member of your family too . . ."
Sounds "A pretty song . . . fascinating and distinctive vocal style . . . lovely . . ."
NME "This is just plain dull. Should be a big hit . . ."
Melody Maker, as well as reviewing the single (" A clever follow–up . . . should be monstrous despite a few cringe–worthy words . . .") lavished Kate Bush fans with a studiously written interview feature by Harry Doherty – a journalist who helped champion the cause for Kate and who has become a good friend in years since.

10th June 1978. *The Man With The Child In His Eyes* enters the charts at number 60.

Topham

1978

17th June 1978. Single up to number 30.

24th June 1978. Up to number 17.

June 1978. The most notable event for Kate this month, despite the immediate success of the follow–up single, was an appearance at Nippon Budokan arena in Tokyo where she performed *Moving* before an 11,000 audience and a TV audience of 35 million for the song festival there. *Moving* was later to be released as her début single in Japan, which easily managed to reach number one.

Kate makes a TV ad for Seiko watches.

July 1978 (Early). *The Kick Inside* slips out of the top 30. Kate returns from Japan to a large EMI party at St. Katherine's Dock near Tower Bridge. For the second LP Kate told the press that she wanted to "become more of a rock singer . . ."

Kate starts work on demos for the next LP at her new home 8–track studio at East Wickham Farm.

4th July 1978. Kate's second single makes the top 10. About *The Man With The Child In His Eyes*, Kate later said to *Ritz*, "I just noticed that men retain a capacity to enjoy really childish games like toys and train sets, all through their lives. Women don't seem to be able to do that . . ."

With the success of *The Man With The Child In His Eyes*, LP *The Kick Inside* moved back up to number eight.

7th July 1978. Kate travels to the south of France to start recording at the Superbear studios in Nice. *Lionheart* LP recording begun as a kind of working holiday on the Riviera. The studio is suggested to her by Dave Gilmour.

At the same time in the US, *The Kick Inside* LP was re–released complete with a re–vamped cover on the new EMI America label. To coincide with this release, *Wuthering Heights*, Kate's first US single was also released but failed to make any impact.

10th July 1978. Kate's recorded appearance on the *Kenny Everett Video Show* broadcast, including a re–edited interview which mixed up all of the questions and answers.

In June the second single – 'The Man With The Child In His Eyes' – was released, again Kate's choice over EMI who wanted 'Them Heavy People'. She felt that 'Wuthering Heights' had been something of a novelty hit and wanted to show she could also handle a straight ballad. The single peaked at number six and helped the album back up the charts again. There was more television, more interviews, various promotional trips abroad. She even made an appearance at the Budokan arena in Tokyo where she performed 'Moving' before a live audience of 11,000 and to a further 35 million on television for a song festival. This later became her first single in Japan and easily reached number one.

Then it was back for an EMI party at St. Katherine's Dock near Tower Bridge (which wag at EMI thought of that one?) followed by several days at her new home studio working on demos for the next LP. She had hardly had time to draw breath since February and now EMI was expecting a new batch of songs. It was a daunting if challenging prospect.

"I learnt very quickly after the first single that if I wasn't careful I could spend twice as much time promoting than actually doing the thing that I was promoting which was the album or whatever. So at that stage I decided it had to be turned around. Promotion is very important but if you're not careful it leaves you shell-shocked and takes you further away from the creative processes. It's just that much harder to get back. Ideally I would just like to work creatively because that's so time-consuming in itself that I still don't think I'd get everything I wanted done."

It must have been a relief when on July 7 they flew out to the south of France to start work on the next album. Producer Andrew Powell remembers, "If you're wandering through an airport or something with her, people would keep stopping her. She actually seemed quite pleased and would not just sign an autograph and throw a bit of paper back at them, she would actually talk to people."

Kate had mixed feelings about being recognised. "Sometimes it's a buzz, being honest, but a lot of the time it embarrasses me, it makes me feel embarrassed with the people I'm with because they get embarrassed. But it's something I'm learning to accept. They're just saying hello in their own way.

"I know a lot of people enjoy it, they really like giving autographs and everything and I think that is important. If anyone asks you for an autograph you must give it to them. I think of myself when I was a kid and saw a star and I thought, 'Oh god!' and I'd really want their autograph. I'd go up and say 'hello' and I'd be so shy. I'd nearly die and I couldn't get the words out. So it is a matter of respect to give that to them because even if they've never liked your music and they've recognised you it's a gesture that I think is nice to give." This respect for her fans is something which clearly inspires the excellent fan club run very much under the auspices of the Bush family. They all write for *The Club* magazine, including Kate, and it publishes many family photos never seen elsewhere.

So in July 1978 Kate ended her teens on the French Riviera, still a little dazed by her success and all it entailed, but with a clear eye to the future.

Gered Mankowitz

LIONHEART

Gered Mankowitz

Left: *From the 'Lionheart' cover session.*

1978

August 1978. Recording at Superbear studios continues. Kate starts to assert herself with greater production ideas, producer Andrew Powell given less space to manoeuvre by his ambitious young artist. *The Kick Inside* still remains in the UK top 20.

5th September 1978. Back in the UK, Kate appears on BBC's *Ask Aspel*. As well as the interview with Michael Aspel, she also performed *Kashka From Baghdad* live on piano.

The rest of the month continued the promotional trail of interviews and appearances. The headlines continued:

The Sun: "Sweet Kate – The Very Private Life Of The Top Twenty Mystery Girl".

Sounds: "Pete Silverton fails to penetrate Wuthering Kate's impregnable niceness . . ."

Kate was also made an interview feature in *Vogue*, complemented by a photo session with David Bailey.

After mixing tracks for *Lionheart*, Kate continued the promotional trail with a tour of Australia and New Zealand. In Australia, Kate appeared on the awards programme, *King Of Pop* on ATV TV (the equivalent to our BPI awards programme). While in Oz she also appeared on Australia's most famous rock programme, *Countdown* hosted by Mollie Meldrum. For this show she premiered her new single to be, *Hammer Horror* having worked out the dance routine just a few hours previous in her hotel room.

27th October 1978. New single *Hammer Horror* reviewed on Radio One show *Roundtable* by DJ's John Peel and Paul Gambaccini (both of whom were unmoved by it) and actress Julie Covington who said; "I think it's wonderful. She writes such extraordinary songs." (Julie, who is a friend of the Bush family, later released a cover version of *The Kick Inside*.)

"I didn't really get on with 'The Kick Inside' very well. For me 'Lionheart' was more of a friend."

Dave Gilmour suggested Superbear studios in Nice on the French Riviera and the recordings for 'Lionheart' were begun almost as a working holiday – away from the 'killer storm' of promotion.

This was to be the last album Andrew Powell would produce for Kate. They still worked together amicably enough but there were more differences this time. As she learned more about the studio she felt she was getting a clearer understanding of how much further she could push her original ideas. Gradually she took more control from Andrew and felt she would soon be ready to step out of another nest. On this album Paddy's skills were also recognised and he played a variety of instruments.

Jon Kelly had been the engineer on the first album at AIR and worked with Kate right through to the third album, which he helped her produce herself. "It was inevitable from the first day of walking into the studio that she enjoyed it so much that she'd eventually end up making her own records, doing completely her own things – producing and arranging and writing and recording all her own albums." Some songs were written in Nice, some had been developed during the crowded past six months and there were a few written before 'The Kick Inside' which had been left out for reasons of space. Really 'Lionheart' marked the end of her teenage, pre-success period, and it would be two years and many changes before the next album.

Asked later how she managed to maintain such a high standard of songwriting she said: "I'd attribute the quality to the fact that I'd written so many songs by the time of my first album, which will probably never happen again unless I don't record an album for a gap of several years. I had five or six years of songs – over 200 – so we had a massive list to choose from. When you are choosing the best you are going to get much better quality. I do feel that the second album suffered just a little because of me not having as much time in between to write and produce new stuff and really sort out the old stuff."

In September Kate was back in London on the promotional trail again. She guested on Michael Aspel's show and played a track from the forthcoming album – 'Kashka From Baghdad'. Perhaps her most prestigious article was an interview in *Vogue* complemented by a photo session with David Bailey.

'Lionheart' was mixed at AIR studios in central London where Kate was still adjusting to her new fame. Producer Andrew Powell remembers, "When we were making 'The Kick Inside' nobody knew who she was so it was quite easy to wander up and down Oxford Street or anywhere else at will, and no-one would recognise her. When we were doing the second record it became harder. She would still offer if we were hungry to go out and get the sandwiches, but we just couldn't let her; we'd have to send somebody out with her."

When the album was mixed Kate took off again for a promotional tour of Australia and New Zealand. The country must have struck her very differently now from her impressions as a child of five or six when the Bush family spent six months there. She always felt a strong response to the primitive force and magic of this rugged continent with its ancient people, the Aborigines, but it would be several years before she felt ready to capture their mood and plight in the studio (on 'The Dreaming').

Meanwhile it was the usual round of pop programmes and interviews and it was in Australia that she premiered her new single-to-be 'Hammer Horror'. "I was quite enchanted by the whole thing of movies and movie sets and ham actors – they're very superstitious places, theatres and movie people . . . " She worked out a dance routine for this performance in her hotel just a few hours before the show!

She returned to Britain for the single release and to prepare for the launch of the new LP 'Lionheart' in November. *New Musical Express*, reviewing 'Hammer Horror' said: "Chilling stuff, ominous post ELO orchestration. The unrequited lust of a broken affair viewed as living dead love-bites-back as in classic fifties celluloid. A real nail biter, hypnotic and disconcerting, catchy as all hell. What exactly are you on Kate Bush? And please can we have some?"

On November 8 Kate attended a private buffet at the Venue in London for the *Melody Maker* Poll Awards. She received awards for Best Female Singer and Brightest Hope Of 1978.

'Lionheart' was released on November 13. *Melody Maker* ran a favourable piece by Harry Doherty to promote the album.

1978

October 1978 (Late). Returns to the UK to make ready for the launch of the next LP, *Lionheart*.

November 1978 (Early). Kate is presented with the Edison Award, the highest accolade that the Dutch Phonographic Industry could supply, in recognition of the outstanding success of *Wuthering Heights*. The event was held at the Kasteel Ammersoyen, a moated 14th century Dutch stronghold near Amsterdam. The event was also used as the international launch of *Lionheart*.

The following day, Kate returned to London to be presented with two awards, for Brightest New Hope and Best Female Singer in the *Melody Maker* readers' poll awards.

Above: *Kate and Cliff promote the LSO's 75th Anniversary.*

"Kate Bush scares me for a combination of reasons. The first is the diplomatic pleasantness and awesome logic she displays in interviews when the initial impact is paired with the multifarious intensity of her music. I start to quiver. The songwriting, the singing, the arrangements, the productions have the mark of a singular personality. Kate Bush's music is more like a confrontation."

The cover shows a bare attic room with Kate in pantomime lion's skin crouching (at bay?) on a packing case. The room is claustrophobic and she may be packed to leave but who knows what secrets lurk within the box. This album is full of fears – fear of dying, of growing up, of failure, love, voices in your head, poison, guilt. And yet the mood of this LP is not one of defeat – Kate's lionheart is challenging the doubts! (She is a Leo.)

The first side launches serenely enough with 'Symphony In Blue', her next philosophy song. Blue is the colour of her room and of the sky between clouds – as if her walls are melting – an exciting and attractive blue which yet induces a kind of vertigo. This fear tempts her to believe in God, but she can't take conventional ideas of God seriously. "I think there are a lot of gods and I certainly believe in my god, but I wonder if it's the same god as yours." But then she sees herself as an essential theme in the world symphony – an Eastern idea expressed in Western musical terms.

Kate's caring childhood gave her a firm base and an instinctive faith in the world . . . but she never discovered where that faith lay – "What is it I believe in?" This song is a step forward from the 'Strange Phenomena' of the last album. Already Kate's philosophy is becoming more personal – there follows a surprising attack on love then praise of sex. Kate is taking refuge in paganism but does she already sense the answer which she is afraid to face? The clue is in an earlier line: 'The meek He seeks, the beast He calms' – this beast is the Hound of Love and it is surely already on her trail.

'Peter Pan' was J. M. Barrie's 'boy who never grew up' and in this next song we plunge back into childhood. Here is a little boy who has been crying all week – 'I no longer see a future' – but why? He has learnt that Peter Pan is not real and that therefore he too will have to grow up. 'They took the game right out of it.' As her brother Jay wrote, "Barrie's bitter, sad condemnation of adulthood has soured many children into seeing growing up as an end to something much more real." Kate had such a magical childhood playing in a farmhouse and its garden among a loving family that, like the Garden of Eden, she doesn't want to leave it. With the logic of childhood and dreams, the child decides 'When I am a man I will be an astronaut and find Peter Pan.' Kate often pairs images of past and present.

This is a song which might make an adult smile but there are darker overtones. Looking in the mirror 'My eyes are full but my face is empty' – did Kate's first awareness of alienation come when she learnt about growing up? 'When you wish upon a star' sounds like Bowie's doom-laden voice in 'The Bewlay Brothers'. (And it was the opening song in Walt Disney's cartoon 'Pinocchio' which inspired Kate in her cover for 'The Kick Inside'.)

Grown-ups and their explanations can be so naive – 'I've been told when I get older that I'll understand it all' – Kate has spent her whole life trying to understand it all and that is the wonder and genius of her work!

1978

3rd November 1978. Single *Hammer Horror/Coffee Homeground* released as a foretaste to LP *Lionheart*.

8th November 1978. Kate attends private buffet at the Venue in London for the 1978 *Melody Maker* Poll Awards. Kate receives awards for Best Female Singer and Brightest Hope of 1978.

11th November 1978 *Hammer Horror* enters the charts at number 73.

13th November 1978. *Lionheart*, Kate's second LP released. *Melody Maker* run another favourable piece to help promote the album, again written by Harry Doherty.

LIONHEART (EMI) EMA 787

Side One
Symphony In Blue
drums and percussion: Stuart Elliot
bass: David Paton
electric guitars: Ian Bairnson
piano: Kate Bush
fender rhodes: Duncan Mackay

In Search Of Peter Pan
drums: Stuart Elliot
bass: David Paton
piano: Kate Bush
acoustic and electric guitars: Ian Bairnson
fender rhodes: Duncan Mackay

Wow
drums: Charlie Morgan
guitars: Brian Bath
bass: Del Palmer
electric guitar: Ian Bairnson
mandolins: Paddy Bush
piano: Kate Bush
synthesizer: Duncan Mackay

Don't Push Your Foot On The Heartbreak
drums: Stuart Elliot
bass: David Paton
piano: Kate Bush
guitars: Ian Bairnson
fender rhodes: Duncan Mackay
hammond: Francis Monkman
slide guitar: Paddy Bush
harmonies: Kate and Paddy Bush

Oh England My Lionheart
piano: Kate Bush
recorders: Richard Harvey
harmonies: Kate and Paddy Bush
harpsichord: Francis Monkman

'Wow' could also be about a Peter Pan – maybe one of Kate's heavy people 'See the diamond glitter through all the rock.' It begins with a thrilling sound like an orchestra tuning up. Here is the adrenalin of performance (or of an audition?) and how people working together hype each other's spirits up with their enthusiasm and admiration. But as most performers know this can be deceptive – 'still we don't head the bill.' And this actor has a problem: many successful performers are gay, but some are too gay – 'will never make *The Sweeney*, be that movie queen. He's too busy hitting the vaseline' – which may hold your hair in place but is better known from pre-Aids days as a sexual lubricant. 'We'd give you the part, my love, but you'd have to play the Fool.' For many gay actors there is no place in the mainstream – we'll call you – 'but don't hold your breath.'

In 'Don't Push Your Foot On The Heartbrake' Kate starts blithely in that little-girl voice . . . but what happens next? After her warnings about 'red love' she is suddenly saying, screaming – 'When you're in love go for it! Don't play it safe!' Speculative philosophy has been dropped in favour of action. Kate is urging this explosive advice so forcefully that it prompts the question whether she is really shouting at herself to give herself courage. But there are other overtones as the 'red glass bleeding' echoes the suspicions of 'Symphony In Blue'.

Soldiers appear frequently in Kate's stories but seldom gloriously. 'Oh England My Lionheart' is a hymn to England sung by a soldier/airman who is dying as the war is ending. He drifts back through his childhood and again we get the image of Peter Pan and maybe the thought that Kate – a Leo – is also saying farewell to the country of childhood. Even a lionheart cannot resist the march of time. 'Don't disturb the clover that grows on the past.' Kate takes war far too seriously to regard it as simply an evocative metaphor, but there is a sense in which she equates it with the profound misunderstanding of one person by another – the war of love. And the Black Spitfire might be Kate's kite in a crash landing.

'Full House' has Kate in another car – maybe it's Emma after successfully controlling her skid. We get a disturbing schizoid image Kate often has of seeing herself outside of herself – and this time running herself over. 'Then the voices begin . . . ' A full-house is a good image for a head crowded with unwanted voices – and a typical one for Kate whose thoughts at this time are seldom far from home. Her advice is fine – 'Stand back and see emotion getting you uptight' – let's hope we remember it when we most need it!

'In The Warm Room' is an intimate gem charged with sexual imagery probably best left to personal interpretation. Kate said in a phone-in interview (February 1979): "I'm always getting accused of being a feminist. Really I do write a lot of my songs for men. 'In The Warm Room' was written for men because there are so many songs for women about wonderful men that come up and chat you up when you're in the disco and I thought it would be nice to write a song for men about this amazing female. I am probably female-orientated with my songs because I'm a female and have very female emotions but I do try to aim a lot of the psychology at men."

The puzzle about this song is the role Kate has adopted – that of a third person predicting intimate events to someone who is not her own lover. Perhaps she is a mother

---

Below Right: *Kate, Janet Brown and Ian Dury at the Capital Radio Music Awards, 1980.*
Far Right: *Collecting her Melody Maker Award from Michael Palin, 1979.*

1978

Side Two
Fullhouse
drums: Stuart Elliot
bass: David Paton
electric guitar: Ian Bairnson
piano: Kate Bush
hammond: Francis Monkman

In The Warm Room

Kashka From Baghdad
drums: Charlie Morgan
bass: Del Palmer
piano: Kate Bush
harmonies, strumento da porco, mandocello and pan–pipes: Paddy Bush
joanna strumentum: Andrew Powell
percussion: Stuart Elliot

Coffee Homeground
rhythm guitar: Ian Bairnson
bass: David Paton
synthesizer: Duncan Mackay
piano: Kate Bush

Hammer Horror
drums: Stuart Elliot
bass: Del Palmer
piano: Kate Bush
electric and acoustic guitars: Ian Bairnson
synthesizer: Duncan Mackay
harmonium: Andrew Powell

Produced and arranged by Andrew Powell, assisted by Kate
Engineer: Jon Kelly
Assistant engineer: Patrick Jauneaud
Assistant engineer on mix: Nigel Walker
Art direction and photography: Gered Mankowitz
Sleeve design: Richard Gray
Front cover concept: John Carder Bush
Make up: Kirsty Climo
Hair: David Kelly
All songs written by Kate Bush
Orchestral contractor: David Katz
Vocals and harmonies: Kate Bush

Kate's sleeve notes: "Special thanks again to dear Dave G, Ricky Hopper, Ma and Pa, Mr Mears, EMI, Hil, Lisa and Rob, Enrico, Harry the Dragonfly and especially Mr P.Pan whose tricks keep us on our toes. And to all of you out there The Lionhearts – do what you will with me, but this is for you. Recorded at Superbear Studios (thank you Damen) and special thanks to Jon Kelly."

speaking these voluptuous lines to a son she is unwilling to release – from Mamma's hand or her own warm room. It would help explain the jarring mention of 'kicking a habit' and 'barricading the way out.' The piano's phrase turning major-minor on 'true' seems to pose a question.

The main piano phrase in 'Kashka From Baghdad' has echoes of Mike Garson's strange piano style on Bowie's 'Aladdin Sane' album. Kate is experiencing alienation again. Cut off from the laughter and love of two men, this time she is not alone in her joylessness. The loving couple are shunned by old friends and never walk abroad in the dark moonlit world. There is one gleam of hope – 'there's light in love you see.' (The little light shining later in 'The Ninth Wave'.)

In the same phone-in Kate explained where the idea came from. "That actually came from a very strange American detective series that I caught a couple of years ago. There was a musical theme that they kept putting in. It was a very moody series and it inspired the idea of this old house somewhere in Canada or America with two people in it that no one knew anything about. And being a small town everyone wanted to know what everyone else was up to, and these particular people in the town had a very private thing happening." (Just so!)

Tom Sheehan

"There is no murder like an English murder." (Alfred Hitchcock). Earlier this century the British public used to take great pleasure in following the great British murder trials, usually in their morning papers. These murders nearly always involved respectable people in claustrophobic suburban houses – family affairs, husbands murdering wives and vice versa. And the favourite murder method was insidious and intimate – poison. The 'loved one' would suffer a painful final illness before burial – sometimes a respectable funeral (followed by a less respectable exhumation) or occasionally, as in the celebrated Crippen case, a hole in the cellar. On 'homeground'.

1978

17th November 1978. Appears on the *Leo Sayer Show* singing *Don't Push Your Foot On The Heartbreak*, pretending at the same time to be digging a hole in the road.

November 1978 (Mid). Carries out a number of personal appearances in record stores around the country.

Actress/singer Julie Covington LP released featuring cover version of *The Kick Inside*, the track dedicated to Kate "for inspiration".

18th November 1978. *Hammer Horror* rises to number 49, but reluctance from Radio One to play the record hampers major sales. The following week the single made number 44 but was doomed from charting higher because of the lack of media coverage and gradually slipped from the charts from then on.

December 1978 (Early). Travels to the States for her second promotional visit.

9th December 1978. Kate makes her first TV appearances on *Saturday Night Live*. The show was hosted that week by *Monty Python's* Eric Idle, who had invited her on to the show. Notably, Mick Jagger also popped by Kate's dressing room to say hello. She performed two songs for the programme, *The Man With The Child In His Eyes* and *Them Heavy People*.

16th December 1978. Due to heavy demand an Official Kate Bush fan club is organised and announced.

December 1978. The Christmas music press summed up the year. Simon Frith of the *Melody Maker* said of Kate:

"Kate Bush's success was a triumph of the romantic will. Her talents are remote, fragmentary, dreams to sustain her house-bound listeners through dark winters to come."

Out of the year, Kate ranked high in the result tables for record sales:
7th best selling LP artist.
The Kick Inside the 10th best selling LP.
Wuthering Heights the 11th best selling single of the year. Kate Bush's first year in the public gaze had come to an end. An unprecedented success by anyone's standards.

'Coffee Homeground' has something of the mood of a Bertold Brecht-Kurt Weill song – cynical pre-war *cabaret* with its spritely German oompah backing and a touch of Lotte Lenya in her voice. The subject matter is as macabre as 'Mac The Knife'.

Coffee is bitter, but if well-sweetened will cover the taste of most poisons. Kate takes a ghoulish delight in toying with this paranoid fear of a lover plotting. (Belladonna means 'beautiful woman'.) It is worth noting the reference to Christie – who hid bodies in a wall cavity and papered them over. And there is an eerie 'preverberation' of the Dennis Nilsen case (1983) – he murdered young men and kept them about the house. She asks about the plumbers going missing and wonders, 'Maybe you are lonely and only want a little company' – Brian Masters' chilling book on these murders was called *Killing For Company*. And it was flesh in the drains that led to Nilsen's discovery. Coincidence or 'Strange Phenomena'?

Below: *Original St Joseph's School magazine covers and promotional photos from the early days.*

Opposite Page: *A rare out-take from the 'Lionheart' cover session.*

34

This album of disturbed people ends in grand style with the *grand guignol* piece 'Hammer Horror', a superb study in guilt. 'Alone on a film set at night with just one spotlight. But who is that in the shadows?' The story is a metaphor for feelings towards a new lover's previous partner. She tells it with great gusto – one of the rewarding things about Kate's music is that even when dealing with problematic emotions and fears she takes such obvious delight in her work! She is never afraid to let loose her sense of humour with such wicked puns as, 'I've got a hunch that you're following to get your own back on me'. This album is full of psychoses but the title seems to say, 'Take courage and face your fears – take heart!'

"I am absolutely fascinated by the states that people throw and put on. It's really fun for me if I can find an area of the personality that is slightly exaggerated or distorted and . . . identify with it to cast a person in terms of that character trait."

The music on 'Lionheart' is accomplished as is the playing – Kate has always been a stylish pianist. But this was by no means all she wanted to do. Despite being a marvellous singer/songwriter/piano-player she would not be satisfied to continue making albums of piano-based songs. She had been working under great pressure but in future she would give herself the freedom to do far more work in the studio and to layer sounds as she layers ideas, not losing that original spark but giving greater depth to the finished recording. The more she learnt about the studio the more possibilities she saw, and the future was boundless.

In December 1978 the Christmas music press summed up the year. Simon Frith of *Melody Maker* said of Kate: "Kate Bush's success was a triumph of the romantic will. Her talents are remote, fragmentary, dreams to sustain her housebound listeners through dark winters to come."

1979

January 1979. Dance and musical rehearsals begin in earnest for Kate's first UK tour. Dance and fitness routines worked out at the Covent Garden Dance Centre; musical rehearsals continued at the Woodwharf Studios in Greenwich.

During this time some new songs are rehearsed at AIR Studios with Kate's old engineer from *The Kick Inside* LP Jon Kelly.

Kate begins stringent dance training under the guiding hand of Anthony Van Laast, principal dancer at the London Contemporary Dance Company. Training is carried out at The Place near Euston.

New year music paper polls released.
NME: Kate polled number three Female Artist and number two Pin-Up.
Sounds: Number three Female Artist, number one New Artist, number two Female Sex Object and number 10 Best Single (*Wuthering Heights*).
Record Mirror: Number two Female Artist, number one New Artist and number three Best Single (*Wuthering Heights*).

January 1979 (Early). In between rehearsals and recording sessions, busy Kate visited the San Remo Song Festival to make her first performance of the new year, which was even televised in Russia.

2nd-4th January 1979. Kate and tour production designer Dave Jackson meet to finalise details for the forthcoming concerts.

8th January 1979. Appears on BBC Radio 2's *Open House* interviewed by Pete Murray.

18th January 1979. Kate and production crew meet up at Woodwharf studios for a script and production meeting. Rehearsals continue at Woodwharf until 24th February.

THE TOUR OF LIFE

LFI

'Amazing . . . incredible . . . fantastic . . . unbelievable . . .'
"Kate and the Bushes wanted something special and anyone who saw the show or the video probably realised it was a bit different to just a band going on the road and playing live." (Richard Ames, tour manager.)

The tremendous success of 1978 had been matched by tremendous pressure. EMI had forced the pace on recording and promotion but when it came to live performance and the first tour Kate was going to take charge. She would not be hurried.

This show had to be very special, more than just another rock concert – even a superb rock concert. Kate knew the stage had more to offer and planned to combine music, dance and theatre, bringing together all the talents and influences she now had at her command.

London was under ice and snow but preparations for the tour began in earnest right from the beginning of January. Rehearsals began at Woodwharf Studios in Greenwich, a few miles from East Wickham farm. It was to be a seven-piece band, based on the KT Bush Band – Paddy, of course, on mandolin and backing vocals, Del Palmer on bass and Brian Bath on rhythm guitar; plus Alan Murphy on lead guitar, Kevin McAlea on piano, keyboards and sax, Ben Barson also on keyboards and Preston Hayman on drums. (Alan and Preston went on to become part of the studio band on subsequent albums.)

This tour was going to be the opportunity – and the acid test – for Kate's abilities as a creative dancer and choreographer. Anthony van Laast was invited in to help her devise routines and train for her performance. They rehearsed at The Place near Euston. Anthony, principal dancer at the London Contemporary Dance Company, was immediately impressed both by Kate and by the plans for the show. She already had firm ideas of what she wanted for each number.

Anthony brought in two dancers, Gary Hurst and Stewart Avon Arnold, and orchestrated what she was doing with them. "Part of Kate's fascination is her idiosyncratic way of moving. So the boys would do a very 'Kate Bush' type performance."

The show would be very elaborate and theatrical with staged routines and extravagant props. Richard Ames was brought in as tour manager to organise the practical side. "Kate and the Bushes wanted something a bit special – it was more theatre, the show was broken up into three acts. From the beginning it was a very long process – I guess the hard work that no one realises was six months of preparation, getting choreographers and dancers, ending up with a 13-piece band."

Over page: *Kate captured at East Wickham Farm by Barry Plummer.*

1979

20th January 1979. Appears on *The Multicoloured Swop Shop*, hosted by Noel Edmonds. Between video clips of *The Man With The Child In His Eyes* and *Hammer Horror*, Kate answered questions from viewers by phone and spoke to the host about her sudden rise to fame and fortune.

Kate's first UK tour was also unofficially announced in some music papers on this day, but exact details of the nature and presentation of the show were kept strictly secret as rehearsals continued.

22nd January 1979. Kate has discussions to plan tour costumes with Lisa Hayes.

February 1979 (Early). *The Man With The Child In His Eyes* released in the US. The single entered the Hot 100 of the Billboard chart on 17th February and peaked at number 85. The first dents in the US charts had been made.

Kate records title song for the film *The Magician Of Lublin*.

18th-21st February 1979. Kate visits Leysin in Switzerland to record appearances for a BBC-inspired European television showcase. The only footage to survive was a video for Kate's following single *Wow*, but this was never broadcast either.

On arrival home from Switzerland, Kate guests on Radio 4's *Woman's Hour* on which she talked, amongst other things, of her fear of dying.

February 1979 (Mid). The national press pick up on Kate's new single, *Wow* giving them further excuses to run hastily-prepared features on the new female sensation.

"Her posturing is blatantly sexual, her hennaed hair is wild and witching, her dress slinky and revealing, her mouth pouting, and her eyes flashing unmistakable signals. The single seems certain to cause a storm when Kate sings it on Good Friday, where all 5' 3', seven-and-a-half stone of her will also be seen flinging her body into wanton erotic gestures." (Gill Martin, *The Daily Express*.)

Bill Duffield

1979

3rd March 1979. Kate Bush's first UK tour officially announced in the music press. Rehearsals extend to Shepperton film studios.

4th March 1979. Kate picks up two new honours in the Capital Radio music awards for Best British Female Artist and Best British Newcomer.

5th March 1979. *Wow* video shown on ITV's *Kenny Everett Video Show*.

6th March 1979. Interviewed on *Thames News* about her forthcoming UK tour.

7th-14th March 1979. Rehearsals continue at Shepperton Studios.
Kate interviewed about the making of the *Wow* video on new BBC programme *Musical Chairs*.

9th March 1979. *Wow/Fullhouse* single released in the UK and rides quickly on the massive promotional campaign engineered by EMI.
Appears on Tony Myatt's Capital Radio show for a short chat about the new single.

13th March 1979. *Wow* arrives in the BMRB charts at number 61.

14th March 1979. Her second interview this month on Capital Radio with Michael Aspel on his morning show. A more general conversation featured including mention of the forthcoming tour.

15th March 1979. Heavy demand for tickets for the tour mean two extra days added at the London Palladium to make up a whole week of performances there. Further dates also added at Manchester and Birmingham.

18th March 1979. Announced that the first UK tour had sold out nationwide.

18th-23rd March 1979. Rehearsals continue at the Rainbow Theatre.

20th March 1979. *Wow* up to number 35 in the charts.

22nd March 1979. *Wow* video screened on *Top Of The Pops*, partly edited by the BBC.

In fact this was a 13-member company: Kate herself, the seven-piece band, two dancers, two vocalists and – a magician! Simon Drake was the "magician, illusionist, mime artist and performer extraordinary". He was at college with Paddy, and Kate's interest in 'strange phenomena' meant an immediate rapport between them.

On March 3 the tour was officially announced and rehearsals shifted to the large film studios at Shepperton. A week later the single 'Wow' (b/w 'Fullhouse') was released with full EMI promotion. Kate appeared on Tony Myatt's Capital Radio show for a short chat. A few days later she mentioned the coming tour on Michael Aspel's morning show, also on Capital. Other interviews followed and on March 18 it was announced that the UK tour had sold out. Other dates were added and they soon sold out too. That day the company secretly moved into the huge Rainbow Theatre at Finsbury Park for the final dress and lighting rehearsals.

There were a few problems with lighting cues so Richard called in Bill Duffield to sort things out. They had worked together with Steve Harley and Peter Gabriel so Bill "brought some of his special magic to the lighting desk". The tour was to open officially on April 3 at the Liverpool Empire but first there was a preview at the Poole Arts Centre near Bournemouth to iron out any last-minute hitches.

Everyone was naturally very nervous but the show went tremendously well and afterwards, Richard recalls, "We went back to the hotel having a few drinks, everyone was very up. And I got the call from the hall that Bill had run back up to the top of the auditorium where the (lighting) desk had been and where he'd been running the show. He was doing the 'idiot check' – you rush up after everything's in the truck just to make sure nothing's forgotten. Someone from the auditorium had lifted up a panel from the flooring on the very last step of the aisle between the seats and placed it on the step below the top step. Bill rushed up, tripped over it 'cos it wasn't lit very well, and went head first down 17 feet onto concrete.

"Bill lasted a week on the life-support machine. Kate was shattered. The whole band, everyone involved – in the short period that people had known Bill, trying to help him as much as possible, he'd pulled off a great show . . . at that point the whole feeling of the tour could have collapsed. I think everyone thought, Bill was a professional like the rest of us and I think any professional would have wanted the thing to carry on and be a success, and we rallied together." So it was decided that the tour would go ahead, and at the end of the tour a special benefit performance for Bill and his parents was arranged at Hammersmith Odeon with Steve Harley and Peter Gabriel.

So on Tuesday April 3, less than 24 hours after the tragedy, came Kate's opening night in Liverpool with all the nerves and adrenalin plus the cold eye of national press and television. Kate was terrified, "not of the audience, but because I might not be good enough. I have been built up over the last year and now I want to give them everything I've got."

The front of the stage was covered by a vast gauze screen, giving a tantalising impression of the stage set and people behind. The electric silence was broken by the eerie sound of whales and the screen surged with glittering green waves which seemed about to engulf the first rows of the stalls. Then as the music rang out a light stabbed from the back of the stage and a tiny figure appeared in silhouette, throwing a huge shadow-figure onto the screen. As she danced forwards the two images merged and the silk swept aside to reveal Kate herself, all shaggy red hair and blue leotard.

'Moving stranger . . . ' the powerful voice soared through the theatre and the audience thrilled with recognition and delight. This unbelievable voice was real, live – here and now! So began what may be the most marvellous and memorable tour it has been any rock fan's fortune to experience.

The set was deceptively simple but effective. The stage was dominated by a huge circular screen like a bamboo-ribbed paper kite. As well as forming a backdrop this was used for projecting slides and film. The bottom of this kite was a circular section which rolled up like a blind to form an entrance, and a metal ramp like a catwalk sloped down from here to centre stage.

'Moving' ended to a roar of applause then more whale whoops introduced the familiar strains of 'Saxophone Song'. These are the first two songs on 'The Kick Inside' (complete with sound effects) and it seemed as if Kate was going to perform the whole album straight through. The number ended with an extended solo, Kevin leaving his keyboards to 'tune in' on his sax. Then over the applause the auditorium throbbed with the sound of a mother's heartbeat and onto the stage rolled a vast metallic egg, the inside padded like a plush red chocolate box. Wedged inside was Kate, rolling over and stepping out to sing 'Room For The Life'.

During the course of the show Kate had *17* changes of costume (dreamed up by Kate and designed by Lisa Hayes). She didn't go offstage for these but disappeared behind her giant egg, which obligingly rolled on and off for her. This was probably one of Simon Drake's devices – he created illusions during several of the numbers and also taught Kate a few tricks. Reviewer Charles Shaar Murray (*NME*) who disliked Kate thought Simon was the real star of the show. So it was unfortunate that he got the magician's name wrong.

The Cast

BEN BARSON
Synthesiser and acoustic guitar

Illusions, magic and mime
SIMON DRAKE

Movement and dance
GARY HURST

ALAN MURPHY
Electric guitar, whistle

Movement and dance
STEWART AVON ARNOLD

PRESTON HEYMAN
Drums and percussion

Mandolin additional instrumentation, vocal harmonies
PADDY BUSH

DEL PALMER
Electric bass

Electric guitar, acoustic mandolin vocal harmonies
BRIAN BATH

Piano, keyboards, saxophone, twelve string guitar
KEVIN McALEA

GLENYS GROVES
Backing vocals

LIZ PEARSON
Backing vocals

1979

24th March 1979. Interview published in *Record Mirror*, the last main interview before the tour, by John Shearlaw.

"It has simply taken all this time to stage things the way I want to. And to match up to the standard I have set myself. . . But however it turns out, it's my concept, as much as the time, the budget and the presentation will allow. It's a culmination of two years planning and six solid months of rehearsal.

"When I'm on stage I get possessed really. Away from it I'm just normal and small, then suddenly I've got this really special thing. I'm really letting go. It's almost like seeing god, man. Though not quite as simple as that."

26th-29th March 1979. Full dress rehearsals at the Rainbow Theatre.

27th March 1979. *Wow* rises to number 23 in the UK charts. By late March, rehearsals have finally ended, and preparations more or less ready for the tour to begin. Final dress rehearsals are completed in secret at the Rainbow Theatre, which was also the culmination of a film report being made by BBC TV's *Nationwide* programme who had been following her rehearsal progress.

2nd April 1979. Kate performs her two-and-a-half-hour set at the Poole Arts Centre in Dorset as a warm-up performance in public for the official opening night in Liverpool. After the successful show, tragedy struck when the lighting engineer for the tour, Bill Duffield fell 17 feet down a hole in the auditorium whilst doing the 'idiot check', ensuring no equipment had been left behind. Kate was shattered and the whole tour was almost cancelled there and then. The decision to continue was only made when it was considered that he would have wanted it that way.

As the egg rolled off stage Kate reappeared in trench coat and fedora looking like a spoof gangster from 'Guys And Dolls' – a pun on 'Them Heavy People'. She was joined by the dancers, Gary and Stewart, two very cute, camp black boys, waving their hands in front of them Jimmy Cagney-style, and the three of them indulged in knockabout fun.

A short intro brought 'The Man With The Child In His Eyes' and a burst of delighted audience recognition. This was followed by 'Egypt', which had not yet appeared on record, with Kate in gypsy attire. Then in 'L'Amour Looks Something Like You' Simon Drake first came into his own, darting about the stage to set mysterious metal balls floating. On this number the backing vocals were very clear (Liz Pearson and Gladys Groves). They were rounded and operatic but less effective than Kate on the original track. The problem of reproducing multi-tracked voice is one of the considerations which has discouraged Kate from live performance. This number ended with a long organ-like synth solo, giving Paddy and a colleague time to clamber into their elaborate 'Violin' costumes for the other new number in the show. Simon donned a crazy spiky wig and fiddled away like a demon on an old violin of Paddy's until smoke poured out of it! So ended the first Act with the violins beating Kate to the ground.

1979

3rd April 1979. Kate's first UK concert tour starts at the Liverpool Empire. The show was a huge success.

4th April 1979. Concert tour continues at the Birmingham Hippodrome. Nationwide TV report is broadcast complete with footage from the first evening's show.

The Daily Mail's Patrick O'Neil reported: "Kate leaves her fears behind and looks like a superstar. She exploded onto the stage a waif-like elfin figure in tight satin jeans and her voice pierced the auditorium with the bewitching quality of the wind shrieking over Wuthering Heights. Like Lisa Minelli, Kate relies not so much on the quality of her voice, but the drama with which she stages her songs."

6th April 1979. Oxford New Theatre.

7th April 1979. Southampton Gaumont.

9th April 1979. Bristol Hippodrome.

The second Act opened with Jay's resonant poetry, then Kate sat alone at the piano for 'The Kick Inside' and 'In The Warm Room'. "I did play two or three numbers on stage – the numbers that I thought were important – but the rest of the time I was way up in front." Yet it sounds uncannily as if Kate is playing on all the songs. "Kevin McAlea was an incredible find because I've never met anyone else who plays the piano – or who *can* play it if he wants to – so like me. Professional pianists tend to *flourish* everywhere, and that doesn't work in my songs because I use a simple style."

Kevin and the rest of the band returned for 'Full House' then an extended intro for 'Strange Phenomena' featured a display of planets on the screen and Simon Drake covering for a costume change. The ramp rose to vertical, displaying a battery of lights, then the boys emerged from under the ramp looking like something between Ziggy Stardust and *Star Trek*, followed by Kate in battered top hat and tails, producing flowers from her sleeve and other conjuring tricks while the boys exclaimed with an exaggerated mime of wonder. The end of the number was extended in a mad seventies thrash.

'Hammer Horror' brought choreographer Anthony van Laast onstage in black-masked executioner's costume. Kate, in widow's weeds and a black veil, was manhandled in a vigorous dance routine – performed to the record. She had courageously (but sensibly) chosen not to sing but to concentrate on the difficult dance – and it gave her a great opportunity for gothic histrionics and facial contortions, rolling her eyes and lashing her tongue in true Hammer fashion.

The band reappeared performing a mad 'Orient Express' steam-engine chant to introduce 'Kashka From Baghdad', the slow performance emphasising the middle-eastern sound of the number. Then 'Don't Push Your Foot On The Heartbrake' set the stage for a street-scene with dustbins, wire-mesh fences and Kate and Co. in shiny black leather waving flashlamps. This is the outfit she wears on the cover of the tour video, except that there she also wears high heels, but she and the dancers were barefoot throughout the show – both for ease of dancing and for costume changes. At the end of this lively number there was a simple but brilliant effect when Gary and Stewart snatched up the dustbin lids and spun them so they resembled racing wheels in the spotlights. (This is one of the clips shown on *The Whole Story* video of 'Wow'.) Then the curtains swung together to end Act Two.

When they swept apart again on the suspenseful first chord of 'Wow' the stage was swirling in dry-ice mist. Kate stood on a catwalk, the ramp raised like a wharf over a misty sea. The two boys were wearing wonderful full white skirts which floated as they spun.

'Coffee Homeground' began with a waltz intro like a fairground organ and Simon Drake appeared as Hugo the Mad Poisoner trying to murder Kate and push her into a big barrel marked 'Pork'. Then more lines from Jay introduced a magical 'In Search Of Peter Pan'. Here Simon transformed to a Puck character with pointed ears – they called this 'Puck rock'! It's amusing to remember that in 1979 most other stages in the country featured young bands spitting and pogo-ing in a very different style of the art of entertainment.

The two bars of 6/8 time at the beginning of 'Symphony In Blue' were also extended as a long waltz intro then a burst of applause came as the number was recognised. After yet another strange waltz section and a few bars of Erik Satie-style piano, Kate took over for a solo rendering of 'Feel It'. (From here on the whole show is shown on the tour video.) 'Kite' brought Kate on in a blue costume with gossamer 'wings', supported in her flight by the boys holding umbrellas with overtones of *Thoroughly Modern Millie* and even *Singing In The Rain*. At the end Simon appeared as a comic airman faking a walking-

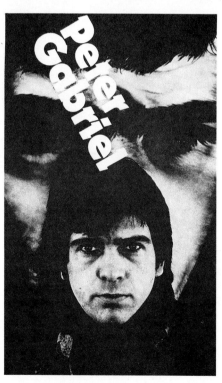

against-the-wind mime. This gave Kate the chance to change into her rhinestone cowboy outfit for 'James And The Cold Gun' when she turned like a spider eating her mate and gunned down every man in sight. For someone whose songs suggest she hates guns she performed all this with great gusto.

This hard rock number was the last one – but not the end of the show. The first encore was 'Oh England My Lionheart' with Kate snuggling inside a huge flying-jacket and the stage strewn with dying airmen and parachute traces. Finally – inevitably – the roar of the crowd brought her back for 'Wuthering Heights', simply performed like the original video. Kate gathered up some of the presents which had sailed over the footlights and ended the night backing up the ramp, waving with great sweeps of her arm as if on a departing liner while the crowd cheered and whistled and clapped along with the heavy snare off-beat as the anthem rolled to its conclusion.

1979

10th April 1979. Manchester Apollo. This performance was filmed by Granada for their rock series *On The Road*. The film made was never broadcast however. *Wow* was benefiting from the publicity generated from the tour and was again rising in the UK charts up to number 14 after dropping to number 27 the previous week. Both of Kate's LPs had also re-entered the charts, both records nestling in the top 30.

11th April 1979. Manchester Apollo Theatre.
Kate picks up the Best Female Singer award for 1978 at the British Rock and Pop Awards. The award was presented to her by Hank Marvin.

12th April 1979. The tour continues at the Sunderland Empire.

13th April 1979. Edinburgh Usher Hall.

15th April 1979. Newcastle City Hall.

16th-20th April 1979. Kate's show opens for a week at the London Palladium.

21st April 1979. Kate is featured singing *Wow* on the *Abba Special*, BBC TV production.
Special benefit show for Bill Duffield announced by Kate Bush for 12th May. Special guests for the show are Peter Gabriel and Steve Harley, old friends of Duffield's.

Over page (inset): *Kate photographed at the Townhouse Studio on her 23rd birthday (photo by Julie Angel).*

There were tears in her eyes as she stepped back through the screen and the theatre curtains swung together. What a tumultuous, glorious success!

After the show there was a very civilized celebration backstage with champagne and vegetarian food (a special chef was booked for the tour) and all the family – the now-extended family – glowing in their collective achievement.

The press was also ecstatic. "The most magnificent spectacle I've ever encountered in the world of rock" Mike Davies, *Melody Maker*. "A dazzling testimony to a remarkable talent" John Coldstream, *Daily Telegraph*. "Quite literally stunning" Thorsen Prentice, *Daily Mail*.

So followed the Birmingham Hippodrome, Oxford New Theatre, Southampton Gaumont, Manchester's Apollo Theatre, the Sunderland Empire and Edinburgh's Usher Hall. The tour came to rest in London on April 16 with a week at the Palladium and a further burst of press praise from those who hadn't made it to the provinces.

On April 24 the European tour kicked off in Stockholm, though Kate's voice was so strained on this occasion that she had to omit the middle 'act'. But the show was still rapturously received.

Right: *Rare programme cover from the Benefit show.*

1979

24th April 1979. Kate's first European concert held in Stockholm at the Concert House.

26th April 1979. Falkoneer Theatre, Copenhagen.

28th April 1979. Tour continues in Hamburg (Congress Centrum).
Song-writing awards, Kate nominated for Best Song Musically and Lyrically (which she won), Best Pop Song (again for *Wuthering Heights*), and Outstanding British Lyric (*The Man With The Child In His Eyes*).

29th April 1979. Carre Theatre, Amsterdam.

2nd May 1979. Leiderhalle Stuttgart.

3rd May 1979. Circus Krone, Munich.

4th May 1979. Guerzerich, Cologne.

6th May 1979. Theatre des Champs Elysee, Paris.

6th May 1979. Mannheim Rosengarten.

10th May 1979. Jahrhunderthalle, Frankfurt.

12th May 1979. A special benefit concert staged for Bill Duffield at the Hammersmith Odeon. The proceeds from the concert went towards a trust fund for Duffield's family. Special guests for the show were Peter Gabriel and Steve Harley, who had both worked with Duffield during their careers.

13th May 1979. Another Hammersmith Odeon show staged, this one videoed and later released. Recordings of the show were also later released on record.

14th May 1979. The last show at the Hammersmith Odeon, the début tour complete.

15th May 1979. An appearance scheduled for *The Old Grey Whistle Test* had to be cancelled because props could not be organised in time.

May 1979 (Late). Kate turns down the offer of writing the theme tune for the new James Bond movie of the day, *Moonraker*. She is busy preparing material for her next LP.

At Amsterdam Peter Gabriel and Steve Harley flew out for a quick rehearsal for the benefit show in two weeks' time. Bill Duffield had provided the lighting on tours for both of them with Richard Ames. Two of Kate's original EMI band had come from Steve's Cockney Rebel. This was the first time Kate met Peter Gabriel and it marked the beginning of a fruitful collaboration.

On Saturday May 12 the company was back in London for the Bill Duffield benefit concert at Hammersmith Odeon. David Lewis reviewed the show for *Sounds*, confessing that he had gone along principally to hear Steve Harley break his two-year silence. But David admitted: "Like practically all the other gnarled old cynics, I cannot deny that I was wrong, her fans were right and she was left to reap the applause for a show that sometimes teetered on the farcical but was never short of compulsive to watch."

The set order had been revamped and it was near the end of the show when Steve and Peter . . . "Crept slowly out of the wings in trench coats and fedoras to singalongaKate on 'Rolling The Ball'." Then after a solo from Steve, he and Peter sang 'Woman With The Child In Her Eyes' as a duet. Later Peter sang 'Here Comes The Flood' unaccompanied and finally Steve Harley had the crowd joining in with 'Best Years Of Our Lives' and 'Make Me Smile (Come Up And See Me)'. As the show ended they were mown down by Kate in 'James And The Cold Gun'. The encore, for Bill, was The Beatles' 'Let It Be'.

Sunday and Monday were the last two nights of Kate Bush's only tour and from them came the video (by Keef Macmillan) which can be seen today. On the last night itself various members of the crew indulged in a time-honoured tradition and arranged a few surprises for Kate.

Richard Ames remembers, "Two of the crew had gone and rented a camel's body, one guy up the neck and another guy on the back legs. Kate started doing 'Egypt' and this camel trolloped on stage. They were only supposed to go on stage for about half a minute just for the laugh but Kate wouldn't let them off. She got hold of the camel's neck and hauled it round the stage singing the whole of the song!"

Pete Still

'Wow' was another 'special' with Kate sitting on a wharf with seaweed hanging from it and dry ice everywhere and the two dancers in long skirts swirling round and round. "The fog and the water gave a great atmosphere. Then from underneath Kate, under the dock, came one of the crew – I think it was the drum-roadie – dressed in complete frogman's outfit – rubber suit, goggles, air tanks, flippers. He came up from under the mist and began dancing with the two dancers in the centre of the stage . . . How Kate didn't stop, it was an incredible piece of professionalism for her, because it was so funny – she should have broken down in complete fits of laughter and she managed somehow to keep going!"

In the audience that night was a young fan Roy who later worked on the *Experiment IV* video. At one point Kate asked for the house lights to be raised for audience shots. "We're videoing this show so tonight we're all stars!"

His final memory is of standing on his seat clapping along with the second encore and thinking, "Why are we all doing this – you can't clap to 'Wuthering Heights'!"

It is doubtful that anyone who bought a ticket for any of Kate's performances left the theatre without a great glow of fulfilment. Yet it is possible to watch the tour video today and feel disappointed. It can all seem a little slow and whimsical to those who have thrilled to Prince's high energy spectacles or been grabbed by the neck by Bette Midler or Tina Turner.

Kate Bush was casting a very different and potent spell. What was special about her right from the start has been her wholly uncompromising attitude – her refusal to stomp along any of rock's easier paths. But it may be that now she is aware of the possibilities opened up by people like Laurie Anderson and Talking Heads, she may feel that any new tour would have to offer far more than even she gave before.

1979

July/August 1979. Kate and new producer Jon Kelly work on the live tapes from the Hammersmith Odeon concert at AIR Studios. Post production work completed by mid-August.

30th July 1979. Kate's 21st birthday.

31st August 1979. Kate's live EP *Live On Stage*, recorded at the Hammersmith Odeon is released. BBC *Nationwide* broadcast the second of their mini documentaries about Kate, together with a new interview recorded at Abbey Road.

16th September 1979. Video prepared for the title track of the live EP, *Them Heavy People*.

23rd September 1979. Guest on Radio 1's *Roundtable* show as a reviewer.

September 1979 (Late). *The Kick Inside* LP is released on picture disc.

9th October 1979. Kate's live EP peaks in the UK charts at number 10.

There is also the question of cost versus venue size. To mount a spectacular show today with all the equipment, without which a gig resembles an Agatha Christie matinee, is staggeringly expensive. So everyone plays the giant stadia – and everyone loses, because these are no places for an artist of any subtlety. Kate would have to think about product endorsement and franchise royalties – but she is more likely to wear a 'Save The Whales' T-shirt than one advertising Cola.

Are these the reasons why Kate Bush has never repeated her success, never toured again – or even performed a live show? She herself might simply say she has been too busy. Writing and recording have always been her main concerns, and as she has become more accomplished at making videos she may feel that this answers the need – producing a better performance and reaching a wider audience.

It may be that she gave a clue when explaining the idea behind 'There Goes A Tenner' which told the story of an unsuccessful bank raid. "For me it's incredibly scary – there's such a potential for something going wrong that it's not worth the risk."

1979

18th November 1979. Appears with Cliff Richard at the Royal Albert Hall in aid of a benefit for the London Symphony Orchestra who were celebrating their 75th year. Performs three songs.

November 1979 (Late). Makes an appearance on the recording of *Sing Children Sing* by Leslie Duncan. Other notables there included the late Phil Lynott, Pete Townshend, Madeline Bell and Joe Brown.
  During this month, Kate's Christmas record, *December Will Be Magic Again* was recorded, but in the event this track was not released until the following Christmas.

22nd December 1979. Kate manages to give a pre-Christmas airing of her festive record, *December Will Be Magic Again* on BBC1's *Christmas Showtime Special*.

28th December 1979. TV special *Kate* broadcast on BBC2, featuring updated versions of *Them Heavy People*, *Heartbreak*, *Child* and *December Will Be Magic Again*. The programme also featured, for the first time, early versions of *Violin*, *Egypt*, *Wedding List* and *Ran Tan Waltz*, tracks soon to appear on the third album *Never For Ever*. Special guest for the show was Peter Gabriel who, as well as performing a memorable version of Roy Harper's *Another Day* with Kate, sung a live version of *Here Comes The Flood*. Their work on this show was to be the first part of a greater collaboration to come.

Left: *Kate with Peter Gabriel at the BPI Awards (LFI).*

NEVER FOR EVER

1980

January 1980. Kate returns to the studio, this time Abbey Road to prepare material for the LP which became *Never For Ever*.

12th January 1980. *Record Mirror* poll published featuring Kate as Best Female Singer and number two for Best Gig.

19th January 1980. Kate top of the *NME* polls with Best Female Artist. Kate also taking this same accolade in *Melody Maker's* year-end poll.

20th January 1980. Sales results for the last quarter issued in *Music Week*, Kate featuring number five Singles Artist, number eight Album Artist and in the awards section she was announced as Best Female Albums Artist for 1979 and number five Best Singles Artist.

25th January 1980. *Games Without Frontiers* single released by Peter Gabriel featuring Kate on backing vocals. (The single later appeared on *Peter Gabriel 3*.) During this time Kate began to experiment with some of the recording gadgets she had been introduced to by Gabriel, notably the Fairlight CMI, the effects of which she later included on tracks like *Babooshka* which featured smashing bottles – the sounds generated by a keyboard from computer disc.

February 1980. Recording at Abbey Road continues for *Never For Ever*. Most of the album was recorded in Studio Two, famed for its historic Beatles connection.

12th February 1980. Kate receives *Music Week* award for Top Female Album Artist at the Dorchester Hotel.

27th February 1980. Kate presented with Best Female Singer award at the British Rock And Pop Awards, the same award she received the previous year. At the same ceremony, Kate presented an absent Gary Numan with his Best Male Singer award.

"She'd been waiting to break out, so I think 'Never For Ever' was where it was going to happen." (Alan Murphy, guitarist.)

The tour ended in May with three shows at Hammersmith Odeon. By the end of the month Kate was already writing material for her next album and during the summer she also worked on live tapes from the tour. This resulted in a live EP with a video for 'Them Heavy People', the main track, which went to number 10. Over the next few months Kate started writing for the next album.

The two years that elapsed between the release of 'Lionheart' (November 1978) and 'Never For Ever' may have seemed an eternity but there are always demands on a successful artist's time and the tour had taken a large chunk of time and energy. In fact by the latter half of 1979 Kate was already recording the new album and the musicians felt as if they hadn't stopped touring but had simply shifted into the studios, again AIR in Oxford Street.

It was important for Kate to be working with familiar musicians because this time she was 'on the other side of the glass'. Andrew Powell was no longer producing and she was sharing this responsibility with Jon Kelly, who had engineered on the first two albums and helped mix the live tapes.

The core of the studio band came from the tour but there were other musicians who came in and fell under Kate's spell. Max Middleton played keyboards and always wore a funny hat. This may seem just a silly joke but in the atmosphere of concentration in the studio anything which breaks the tension is welcome.

Again Paddy played a wide selection of foreign and ancient instruments – balalaika, sitar, koto, strumento de porco, musical saw, mandolin and the humble harmonica. But Kate found a new toy which soon became one of her greatest tools – the Fairlight. She had met Peter Gabriel when they did the Hammersmith show for Bill Duffield and this became the first of many collaborations; he guested on her BBC TV Christmas show and the following month she did backing vocals on his singles 'Games Without Frontiers' and 'No Self Control'. Peter introduced her to drum-machines and to the Fairlight CMI.

This is a computer which can 'sample' a recorded sound and then by varying the pitch and other characteristics turn it into a scale of musical notes which can be played on a keyboard. A good example of this is the sound of breaking glass on 'Babooshka'.

It is an ideal instrument for her cinematic approach to music. "Although the Fairlight is called a synthesizer so many of its sounds are actually of a natural source," she says.

"That's why I like it so much. The Fairlight seems to be a huge bridge between all kinds of music." On this album Duncan Mackay programmed and played the Fairlight but by 'The Dreaming' she had learnt to play it herself.

"The great thing with the Fairlight is I can write a piece on it with an acoustic guitar or a cello then I can get a musician in to play that, so he's playing what I've written, but much better. (Then I can) use the Fairlight to do something to complement him. It's the blend of two worlds – I find that fabulous."

In 1980 she moved to EMI's own studios at Abbey Road (where The Beatles used to record). This may have been prompted by the cost of recording. As she enjoyed the greater freedom of producing herself she found her painstaking approach was taking far longer than before.

The first release of any of this new work was 'Breathing' in April of that year. This displayed Kate's new-found command of the studio and marked a new departure in her writing.

The controversy which surrounded 'Breathing' and its accompanying video meant she had scored a bullseye with her first shot. She had seen a documentary about the aftermath of nuclear war and had found a personal way to confront this issue.

Express Newspapers

Kate said in an interview later, "I think 'Breathing' is about violence just because it's so negative. And yet people seem to treat it on just a normal level. This baby that's being born has had perhaps several lives before ('I've been out before but this time it's much safer in') and is about to be destroyed inside its mother. It's living off its mother and its mother will die before it sees a day of life." (This track has recently been included on a Greenpeace anti-nuclear album.)

This single went to number 16 and was followed in June by 'Babooshka' which reached number 5 and went silver, her best-selling single since 'Wuthering Heights' – despite the fact that the lively video was hardly seen owing to a TV strike.

'Never For Ever' finally appeared in September, almost two years after 'Lionheart'. 'Army Dreamers' was released as the accompanying single, coupled with 'Delius' and 'Passing Through Air', a pretty but very straightforward love song written in Kate's early teens and demoed in Dave Gilmour's studio in 1973.

The cover is a painting by Nick Price showing barefoot Kate in a frock like a window in the sky – 'blue between clouds'. The skirt billows like a cornucopia from which bursts a host of creatures, some benign but many grotesque and disturbing. Kate, with her arms above her head and only slight surprise on her face, is finally releasing the demons which threatened her lionheart. The back cover is a wonderfully gothic flight of Kate-bats with red tongues.

1980

29th February 1980. Kate makes a surprise appearance on Delia Smith's cookery programme, talking to the host about her vegetarian lifestyle and favourite food dishes and recipes.

1st March 1980. *Sounds* poll published, Kate making the top again with Best Female Singer – the fourth music paper to declare the same result this year.

3rd March 1980. London's Capital Radio awards ceremony held at the Grosvenor Hotel, Kate picks up, what else but the Best Female Singer from Kenny Everett.

March 1980. *The Unknown Soldier*, an album by Roy Harper released which featured a duet with Kate on one track, *You (The Game Part II)*. Roy Harper had asked Kate to appear on his album after being introduced to her work by Kate's old friend Dave Gilmour. (Session recorded in January.)

This same month an unusual film was put on commercial release entitled *The Magician Of Lublin*, taken from the novel by I.B. Singer. The theme tune *The Magician* had been sung by Kate but this failed to save its life and it was withdrawn soon after release. A hoped-for soundtrack record of the theme and score was never released.

March 1980 (Late). Announced that Kate's next single to be *Breathing/The Empty Bullring*.

7th April 1980. Kate is featured as special guest on the *Dr Hook* BBC2 special by special request of the band. Kate performed what was to have been the proposed next single, *Babooshka*. (Kate's appearance recorded the month before.)

Top Left: *Kate on stage with Bob Geldof at the 1987 Amnesty International concert.*

Bottom Left: *Kate and admirer photographed at the Video Cafe Party,* (**Photos:** *this page Julie Angel; opposite, David Redfern*).

'Babooshka' is a delightful romp with a serious heart – a philosophical and psychological knot. It may be incidental but 'Babooshka' is the Russian 'Mother Christmas'. She travels the world with a sack full of toys giving one to every child she finds in the hope that one may be the infant Jesus. Among the toys might be those Russian dolls which fit inside each other so you never know when you've got to the last one. Inside everyone there may be their younger self trying to get out. Is the husband being unfaithful? – is the wife? Each of them declares 'All yours!' but are they really? Do we ever know the one we love, what they are really like inside? Kate will return to this question more passionately in 'Running Up That Hill'.

A drummer called Roland is credited with percussion on 'Delius'. In fact Roland is the name of a Japanese instrument firm that made an early drum-machine/rhythm-box which provides the gentle Latin beat beneath this song.

Frederick Delius (baptised Fritz but born in Bradford) was a very English composer of such songs and orchestral pieces as 'On Hearing The First Cuckoo In Spring'. Like Kate he drew on English folk songs for inspiration. In later life he became blind and largely paralysed so he could no longer write his music. In the 1930s the young Eric Fenby devoted part of his life to Delius, writing down his music from dictation. ('In B Fenby.') This beautiful little number is surely a wry comment on her earlier problems in the studio getting what she wanted down on record while working with a producer who didn't always understand her.

1980

11th April 1980. Kate's new single *Breathing* discussed on Radio One's *Roundtable* show, the panel featuring Ian Dury, Anne Nightingale and Kid Jensen, all of the panel decidedly moved by the power of the track – which Kate had pushed for release in front of *Babooshka*.

Breathing received a critical reception from the music press but left Kate undaunted, the single was an important milestone for her and was born after she had seen an in-depth documentary about the aftermath of nuclear war.

14th April 1980. *Breathing/The Empty Bullring* single released.

22nd April 1980. *Breathing* enters the BMRB charts at number 44.

24th April 1980. Guests on the Kid Jensen show for the evening, playing her favourite records of the moment (BBC Radio 1).

25th April 1980. Guests on Radio 1 again, this time with Anne Nightingale, mentioning the pressures she was under to finish her new album on time.

29th April 1980. *Breathing* rises to number 29 in the UK charts.

Kate appears on *Nationwide* BBC TV programme to talk about the reasons for releasing a single like *Breathing* and her general views on the subject. Most of her controversial video was shown on the programme, as against shows like *Top Of The Pops* who only showed the opening section.

April 1980. Interview for German television filmed in the UK. The completed 45-minute film included sections from some of Kate's live German performances.

6th May 1980. *Breathing* rises to number 24 in the UK.

10th May 1980. Kate attends Convention for the Official Kate Bush Club held at the Empire Ballroom, Leicester Square.

Photo: *Kate and double bass captured by Tom Sheehan.*

Tom Sheehan

'Blow Away', dedicated to Bill Duffield who died on the first night of the tour, is the strangest of Kate's philosophical songs. It is a whimsical reflection on death. Does a musician's music die with the body or live with the soul? On a phone-in programme she said, "I don't see how anyone can really say what happens when our body dies. There's no way of knowing where the energy goes."

Here Kate describes the Near Death Experience when someone seems to leave their body and make contact with people 'on the other side' – but then returns to life. This feeling is supposed to be very calm, not frightening, and Kate imagines saying hello to Minnie Riperton, Keith Moon, Sid Vicious, Buddy Holly, Sandy Denny and Marc Bolan – an eclectic band!

'Egypt' is an evocative country with its history of god-kings and magical rites performed under a fierce sun – a history which was entombed for thousands of years only to be resurrected in recent times. Kate seems to be taking Egypt as a symbol for her body while in the second verse her sexuality is a cat. The cat, sacred to the ancient Egyptians, is an appropriate image – her movements are feline and with those high cheekbones and strong Irish upper lip you can imagine her sporting elegant shiny whiskers and cleaning them with a contented purr!

Pictorial Press

Side two starts with another of Kate's macabre romps. 'The Wedding List' may have come straight out of a newspaper – but was the whole story there or did she read about the first killing and dream up the revenge to get something out of her system? At school Kate filled in a mock questionnaire and against the question married? she put "Definately (sic) not!" The chorus sounds strangely sweet, but then Kate is at her most dangerous when she sounds sentimental.

'Violin' is a grotesque romp with Kate delighting in her word play – 'quivers', 'bow', 'quavers', 'bar' etc. It has images of leaving – 'over the bridge,' 'out of the orchestra'. If it's not too fanciful this may be Kate having a wry dig at the violin she learnt at school but didn't enjoy. Paganini was the first real violin virtuoso. He was supposed to have sold his soul in a Faustian pact with the devil ('old Nicky') in return for his demonic talent. Nero was the mad emperor who fiddled while Rome burned.

'The Infant Kiss' is about a woman with a child in her eyes, and the very difficult subject of child-love. There is a sense in which no child has the responsibility to consent, but it does not follow that no child wishes to – 'Let go!' has two very different meanings. 'I must stay and find a way to stop' conveys how temptation can twist logic. 'Knock knock who's there in this baby?' Babooshka in reverse.

Over page: *Kate pictured at the press launch of 'Hounds of Love' (LFI).*

1980

15th May 1980. *Smash Hits'* interview with Kate published, written by Deanne Pearson: "There are a lot of different songs with no specific theme, but they're saying a lot about freedom which is important to me."

20th May 1980. *Breathing* reaches its highest chart position at number 16.

30th May 1980. Peter Gabriel's third solo album released featuring the successful *Games Without Frontiers* and *No Self Control*, both tracks featuring Kate on backing vocals.

June 1980. *Babooshka/Ran Tan Waltz* single released to help amend the delay in Kate's third LP which, it was thought, would be put back to early September.

1st July 1980. *Babooshka* enters the UK charts at number 63.

8th July 1980. *Babooshka* jumps to number 16 in the UK.

15th July 1980. *Babooshka* peaks at number seven, where it remains for two weeks. (The single made number one in Australia.)

19th August 1980. *Babooshka* receives a silver disc for UK record sales. At this time it was Kate's second biggest selling single.

25th August 1980. *Babooshka* enters the Australian charts at number 30.

29th August 1980. Guests on BBC Radio 1's *Roundtable* as fellow critic with Paul Gambaccini and Paul Burnett.

30th August 1980. Interview published in *Sounds* by Phil Sutcliffe, one of Kate's most open interviews to date.

September 1980. Kate flies to Munich to make an appearance on West German TV's *Rock-Pop*, performing *Babooshka* and *Army Dreamers*. While in Germany Kate is also interviewed for a feature-length article in *Melody Maker*.

Pat Benatar releases *Crimes Of Passion*, an LP which features an interesting cover version of *Wuthering Heights*.

A strange sound (violin harmonics? wind in telegraph wires? fingertips on wine glasses?) leads into 'Night Scented Stock', described as an instrumental with possibly unintentional accuracy. Kate uses her voice skilfully as a collection of instruments to play a nocturne – maybe a keyboard sonata on the Fairlight.

In 'The Infant Kiss' she saw the adult in a child. On 'Army Dreamers' she sees the child classified as adult but never making it. 'Poor old ego, trying to find a way to be butch and brave only to find reality is the challenge.' In this pretty little waltz her voice is at its sweetest and most ironic as she coldly condemns the system which uses false dreams to lure unemployed teenagers into the macho world of death. This is the voice of a mother, not blinded by tears but seeing all too clearly the mockery of the waste of life. She underpins the song's atmosphere with the sounds of barrack square bawling and a rifle bolt being pushed home.

With this song and the final track 'Breathing' Kate showed she was fully ready to tackle difficult and contentious subjects – and tackle them with consummate skill and a very individual voice. Politics must be the hardest subject for pop to embrace without sounding trite. But she is writing from the heart and goes straight to the heart of the matter. Her irony is as sharp as Dylan's ever was and if 'Blowing In The Wind' planted seeds which may have helped turn opinion against one war let us hope that Kate's message will not fall on stony ground.

On this album Kate gets many demons out of her system – with anger and with humour. Many of the songs are concerned with loss – of identity, faculties, life, faith, and innocence. But as on 'Lionheart', she is never negative in her response. In one of her earliest interviews she said: "If you're writing a song then you have a responsibility to people. It's important to give them a positive message. Something that can advise or help is far more effective than having a wank and being self-pitiful." She may not know in what her faith lies but she will do her best to pursue it and hammer it out.

'Never For Ever'. . . the album's title and cover evoke a fairy-tale mood. The moral of these tales is, there is nothing you cannot change if you try hard enough. Appropriately this was her first album to reach number one – and the first ever by any British solo female singer.

Previous page: *Kate with long-time boyfriend Del Palmer (LFI/Julie Angel).*
Insets: *Kate and Del on 'The Big Sky' video shoot.*

1980

8th September 1980. *Never For Ever*, Kate's third LP released. The day spent conducting interviews for Radios 1 and 2 and Capital Radio. The album immediately rose to number one in the charts.

During the same week of the release of the LP, Kate attends a Stevie Wonder concert in London, the show inspiring her to write *Sat In Your Lap*.

NEVER FOR EVER (EMI) EMA 794

Side One
Babooshka
drums: Stuart Elliot
electric bass: John Giblin
Fender rhodes: Max Middleton
balalaika, backing vocals: Paddy Bush
electric guitars: Brian Bath, Alan Murphy
backing vocals: Gary Hurst
C.S.80: Kate Bush

Delius (Song Of Summer)
percussion: Roland
Delius, sitar: Paddy Bush
electric guitar: Alan Murphy
bass voices: Ian Bairnson, Paddy Bush
additional percussion: Preston Heyman

Blow Away (for Bill)
drums, percussion: Preston Heyman
fretless bass: Del Palmer
Fender rhodes: Max Middleton
acoustic guitar: Brian Bath
strings: The Martin Ford Orchestra
string arrangement: Max Middleton

All We Ever Look For
Koto: Paddy Bush
acoustic guitar: Alan Murphy
acoustic guitar: Brian Bath
Yamaha C.S.80: Kate Bush
timpani: Morris Pert
fairlight: Duncan Mackay
backing vocals: Preston Heyman, Paddy Bush, Andrew Bryant, Gary Hurst

Egypt
drums, percussion: Preston Heyman
electric bass: Del Palmer
Fender rhodes, mini-moog: Max Middleton
strumento de porco, backing vocals: Paddy Bush
prophet 5: Mike Moran

Pictorial Press

THE DREAMING

" 'The Dreaming' was much more of a night-time album – I'd normally do my vocals in the evening."

In September 1980 'Never For Ever' was pipped at the number one position after only one week by Bowie's 'Scary Monsters' but still went gold by November. That month Kate went to a Stevie Wonder concert which had a similar effect on her music to that which Lindsay Kemp had on her performance. The very next day she put down a demo of 'Sat In Your Lap', and the energetic drum-based style gave her the key to a new way of composing. This would bear fruit on the LP she was about to begin.

Kate spent most of her time between the release and the end of the year promoting the album and the singles 'Army Dreamers' and 'Babooshka'.

'December Will Be Magic Again' was duly released for Christmas having just missed the date last year. The first verse is a humdrum Christmas mixture but the chorus harks back to 'Kite' with Kate floating down like a snowflake. In the second verse – 'Light the candle lights to conjure Mister Wilde' – she settles down in her den with a Christmas present: *The Complete Works Of Oscar Wilde* perhaps, published in 1976.

The B-side, 'Warm And Soothing' is a gentle but unsentimental portrait of an elderly married couple with Kate wondering how her ideas of love will weather in old age. The wayward melody and simple piano accompaniment hark right back to 'In The Warm Room' and other tracks on 'The Kick Inside', but it was recorded during the making of 'Never For Ever'. " 'Warm And Soothing' was a demo tape which we did basically just to see what Abbey Road sounded like. We wanted to work there and we went into Studio Two and really the only way we could tell if it was going to sound good was if I went and did a piano vocal. So I did and it sounded great."

This single was popular on the radio but only made number 29 in the charts. Everyone's Christmas magic was overshadowed by John Lennon's murder that year.

Left: *From an unusual photo session with Anton Corbijn in 1983.*

1980

Side Two
The Wedding List
drums, percussion, backing vocals:
Preston Heyman
bass: Del Palmer
electric guitar: Alan Murphy
electric guitar, backing vocals: Brian Bath
Fender rhodes: Max Middleton
strings: Martin Ford Orchestra
string arrangement: Max Middleton
harmonica, musical saw, backing vocals:
Paddy Bush

Violin
drums: Preston Heyman
electric bass: Del Palmer
electric guitar: Brian Bath
electric guitar and solo: Alan Murphy
violin: Kevin Burke
banshee: Paddy Bush

The Infant Kiss
viol: Adam Sceaping
lironi: Jo Sceaping
electric guitar: Alan Murphy
string arrangement: Jo and Adam
Sceaping

Night Scented Stock

Army Dreamers
bodhran: Stuart Elliot
acoustic guitar, backing vocals: Brian
Bath
backing vocals, mandolin: Paddy Bush
backing vocals, electric and bass acoustic
guitar: Alan Murphy
fairlight: Duncan Mackay

Breathing
drums: Stuart Elliot
fretless bass: John Giblin
Fender rhodes: Max Middleton
electric guitar: Alan Murphy
electric guitar: Brian Bath
prophet: Larry Fast
percussion: Morris Pert
backing vocals: Roy Harper

Over page: *Costume fitting for 'Experiment IV' at Pinewood Studios. Photos by Roy Puddefoot and Geoff Portass. (Dresser Tina Earnshaw pinning Kate's hair.)*

Previous page: More Pinewood shots. Geoff Portas with paint brush while Charles Knode (costume designer) looks on.

1980

Produced by Kate Bush and Jon Kelly
Engineer: Jon Kelly
Assistant engineer at Abbey Road
Studios: John Barrett
Assistant engineer at AIR Studios:
Jon Jacobs
Art direction: Kate Bush
Front cover and centre: Nick Price
Back cover concept and photography:
John Carder Bush
Lettering: Carol Bennett
Costume design: Gini Hardy
Artwork co-ordination: Paul Maxwell Ltd
All songs written, and except where
stated, arranged by Kate Bush
Vocals, piano and harmonies: Kate Bush

Kate's sleeve notes; "Special thanks to
Paddy for all his ideas; to Richard
Burgess and John Walters for bringing in
and programming the Fairlight, CMI, and
for their warmth and enthusiasm; Max
Middleton for all his help; Kevin McAlea
for his ingenuity and for playing me
Chopin; Herbie Flowers for making me
feel happy; Roy Harper for holding on to
the poet in his music; Peter Gabriel for
opening the windows; Hannah and Jack
for being there; Krishna and Ranchor for
showers of gifts; and to Richard Ames,
Jeremy Andrew, Eddie, Lisa, Vera, Hil, Bill
and Tell, John, John, John, Jon, Jon and
to all the musicians who have worked
patiently and understandingly on this
album to make it the way I always wanted
it to be."

6th September 1980. Reviews for *Never
For Ever* are published in the music
papers.
    Paul DuNoyer for the *NME* wrote:
"Her finest achievement to date, a work
of ingenious exquisite modern MOR of
the very highest refinement and delicacy,
but it's perfection in a vacuum. Kate
Bush's newest writing displays a pure
melodic gift to rival any but McCartney's.
It's MOR, it's show business, it's
dishonest."
    Tony Mitchell for *Sounds* wrote:
"This album has been a long time in the
making, but I'm not sure that this is
always a good thing. I can't honestly
claim to have been moved by this album
as I'd hoped."

In March she went into her own home studio to start writing for the next album, recording the results on her eight-track machine. In May full recording began at Abbey Road studios and her demos were transferred to the big multi-track as guide tracks. With no tour to think of and a minimum of promotional work Kate was able to spend plenty of time writing the songs. "It took about four or five months as I wanted a big selection of songs to choose from. I thought it was only going to take a couple of months but before I knew it the whole thing was becoming more involved and I knew it was going to take me at least six months to a year to get it the way I want."

With full command of the studio, she was producing this album alone. She used different engineers in the different studios so no-one was 'holding her hand' now. (Engineers tend to stick with their studios as they know their equipment.) Most of this album was recorded at EMI's Abbey Road, the number three studio, small and intimate with the control room overlooking the studio below.

Now Kate had control, work for this LP was far more experimental than before, seeds of ideas being developed with whichever instruments and musicians seemed most appropriate rather than simply layering over a piano-based song.

"Each track has a different mood and it was nice to use people almost specifically for what they were very good at. Jimmy (Bain) is a simple rock 'n' roll player and what the whackier tracks needed was a very simple driving bass to keep the whole thing going without being distracting."

That summer 'Sat In Your Lap' gave a taste of the LP that was still more than a year away, reaching number 11 in the charts. It was Kate's first solo production and showed a marked development in her writing and recording skills and gave warning of the LP to follow. The B-side, 'Lord Of The Reedy River' was a folk-style song of Donovan's and was one of her choices on the Paul Gambaccini show the previous December. ("Special thanks to Donovan for writing such a beautiful song.") In October the video of Kate live at Hammersmith Odeon was released. Work continued on the album until the final mix in May 1982. Then Kate took a much-needed holiday in Jamaica.

Express Newspapers

In July Kate was called on at two days' notice to take David Bowie's place in the Prince's Trust Royal Gala at the Dominion Theatre. She performed 'The Wedding List' with a band consisting of Pete Townshend and Midge Ure on guitars, Mick Karn (Japan) on bass, Gary Brooker (Procol Harum) on keyboards and Phil Collins on drums. During the number the strap of her dress broke and she ended her performance clutching her bosom and improvising choreography.

At the end of the month the single 'The Dreaming' was released. The reviews were excellent, praising Kate's courage, but BBC's Radio One thought differently and it didn't make the playlist. As a result it only reached 48. Apparently EMI had lost faith and didn't plug the record properly. With an eye on the enormous studio costs they decided not to throw more money after it and simply allowed it to 'escape' – music biz jargon for an unsupported release. They also found the album incomprehensible. The music was nothing like the pure pop of Dollar who typified the state of the charts. "Everyone felt it was uncommercial and so *different* – 'Oh, what a lot of time you've spent in the studio, Kate!' And there were no hit singles."

Had Kate been out of the limelight too long – especially as she was recording such uncompromising material? When she started the album she felt she had barely finished promoting 'Never For Ever' and the singles, but . . . "By the time it's finished I've been out of the public's eye – apart from 'Sat In Your Lap' which got to number 11, but they forget about that – they forget that ever happened."

At the time this must have seemed to be a major problem, and 'There Goes A Tenner' was quickly released as a more commercial bid for the charts. But EMI didn't even bother to plug this and it simply failed to register.

Kate didn't share EMI's doubts. In an interview with Peter Nash at the time she said (of 'The Dreaming'), "For a song that didn't get any higher than number 40 it got an incredible amount of feedback! If I had to release a song again at that time I'd release that again. I don't feel any regrets at all." Maybe this was because the album had just reached number three!

Pictorial Press

1980

9th September 1980. Kate travels to Edinburgh for interviews and public appearances in the city, and then on to Glasgow for more of the same.

10th September 1980. Kate visits Newcastle-upon-Tyne, appearing in the Virgin record store in Eldon Square.

11th September 1980. PAs continue in Manchester and Birmingham.

12th September 1980. Kate appears at the Virgin Megastore signing copies of her album, the final leg of her mini UK promo tour.

16th September 1980. *Never For Ever* reaches number one in the UK charts.

22nd September 1980. *Army Dreamers/Delius/Passing Through The Air* single released. (It had been rumoured that *Army Dreamers/Violin* would be a possible double A-side release.) *Passing Through The Air* had originally been written a few years earlier and demoed with Dave Gilmour and the two session players from a band called Unicorn whom Gilmour was also encouraging at the time.

23rd September 1980. *Never For Ever* is pipped at the number one album position after only one week by David Bowie's *Scary Monsters* but the record had already gone gold.

26th September 1980. Mick Jagger speaking about Kate Bush on Radio 1's *Roundtable* commented; "She's very nice. I don't really like this particular record *Army Dreamers*, it's not my kind of music. I pass."

30th September 1980. *Army Dreamers* arrives in the UK charts at number 57.

October 1980. Kate works on a video presentation of *Army Dreamers*, making what she later considers her most successful video to-date.

Kate is no longer singing to us from the piano – she is whispering (and shouting) inside our head. She is confident to let the music stand on its own, building from a firm foundation which sets the rhythm and mood. That was important because 'The Dreaming' is a set of dreams and states of mind.

The cover shows Kate as a very glamorous Mrs Houdini ready to pass a tiny golden key from her mouth to that of her manacled husband. Houdini was the great escapologist of this century and this method was one of his tricks. Kate is wearing a houndstooth tweed jacket and two black bands of ribbon on the sleeve make it look as if she too is manacled. Locks and keys also have sexual connotations in many folk songs.

Right: *Harry Houdini about to be lowered into the Charles River, Boston, 1906. (Is that Mrs Houdini in the background?)*

1980

4th-10th October 1980. BBC2 *Rock Week* features Kate's Keef Macmillan film of her performance at the Hammersmith Odeon which, apart from a screening at the Kate Bush fan club convention, was the first time it had been publicly screened.

Melody Maker announce that Kate has topped their annual poll for the third year running – Best Female Singer. This same week, Kate receives her award from Rowan Atkinson at a *Melody Maker* party. She later returned the compliment by presenting him with a gold disc for sales for the LP of *The Secret Policeman's Ball*.

13th October 1980. Kate works on mixing the track *Warm And Soothing* before travelling to Europe for a brief promo tour.

14th October 1980. Conducts various interviews for the Australian press.

15th October 1980. Travels to Holland to record an appearance performing *Babooshka* and *Army Dreamers*.

16th October 1980. Visits Munich and Hamburg for press and radio interviews to promote the new album.

After returning to the UK briefly, Kate then travelled to Venice, again performing *Babooshka* on Italian TV and further promotion. The single goes top ten in Italy, in West Germany making the top 30.

Behind the entwined couple is a background of ivy which also covers the reverse of the album sleeve. Brewer's *Dictionary Of Phrase And Fable* (a fascinating reference book) tells us: "In Christian symbolism ivy typifies the everlasting life from its remaining continually green." 'Houdini' is about a final attempt to cheat death and 'The Dreaming' is about Aborigines facing the extinction of their culture. Two years later the B-side 'Under The Ivy' suggests that for Kate ivy represents privacy and secrecy – there is a lot of it in the family farmhouse garden!

'Sat In Your Lap' bursts out with great urgency as Kate tackles philosophy again – with a vigour which suggests she feels she ought to have solved the riddle by now! But she ridicules her own impatience. The writing here is direct and vivid. She tells the story of her search for the answer as concisely as if she were writing prose, but the poetry says much more. 'Some say that knowledge is something sat in your lap' – and we see someone meditating in lotus posture. Or a child – 'All we ever look for'.

For most people it is enough to work and not think. If some people can be happy why not me? The truth is so elusive – just when you think you've grasped it it slips away. Some say the answer is in laughter – or they laugh at it. 'Some say knowledge is something that you never have.' But Kate is not giving up. The answer may be elusive but she suspects it is always right there before you if you can only see. You don't need a jet to Mecca (a centre of religious 'knowledge' like Tibet, Jeddah, Salisbury). Babooshka and her husband were so close to it. The key is in your mouth. I *will* find it – 'I'm climbing up the ladder!'

'There Goes A Tenner' has Kate telling a funny but cautionary tale. She thinks it's wrong that burglars and safebreakers are always portrayed as cool customers – surely they must be frightened and make silly mistakes sometimes? "I always thought that if I ever did a robbery I'd be really scared – I thought that's a much more human point of view."

'Pull Out The Pin' – in two bars Kate has transported us to the steaming green of South East Asia, another country and another state of mind. This does not feel like a written song so much as a mood that has coalesced. Kate has woven a jungle backdrop of sound effects, the squeaking of insects, the jangling of nerves. "The Vietnamese who were fighting the Americans were Buddhists, and they would pop a little silver Buddha in their mouth before they went into battle so if they died they'd have Buddha on their lips.

There's such irony throughout history between religion and war." This gook is not a foreign body to line up your sights on. No – here I am on my belly stalking the American 'child', so aware of his smell and his physical presence that we could almost be lovers. The pin is pulled in the first minute of the song and all the thoughts take place in that endless moment before death explodes.

May I have the pleasure? – now Kate whisks us off for a dream in fast waltz time. 'Suspended In Gaffa' is distinctly reminiscent of Gilbert and Sullivan's 'Nightmare Song' from 'Iolanthe': 'Well this you can't stand so you throw up your hands/And you find you're as cold as an icicle/In your shirt and your socks – the black silk with gold clocks/Crossing Salisbury Plain on a bicycle.'

Julie Angel

Left: *Kate and Gary Glitter at the Secret Policeman's Ball.*

1980

20th October 1980. *Babooshka* makes number one in Australia.

21st October 1980. *Army Dreamers* rises to number 16 in the BMRB charts.

28th October 1980. *Army Dreamers* peaks in the UK charts at number 14.

November 1980. *Never For Ever* LP goes gold in the UK. *Flexipop* magazine feature an article written by Kate, her diary of events between the dates 29th August to 4th September 1980.

3rd November 1980. *Babooshka* having been toppled from the number one position in Australia by Leo Sayer, again claims the premier position.

4th November 1980. *Army Dreamers* at number 17 in the UK charts.

November 1980 (Mid). *December Will Be Magic Again/Warm And Soothing* single released, the song Kate had rushed to record for the Christmas of 1979 finally found a release date, but was accordingly revised – making the most of the 12-month delay forced upon it.

Kate and Peter Gabriel work together in the studio. No material is released from this liaison.

The clues are in the chorus – 'My feet are feet of mud, it all goes slow-motion, I don't know why I'm crying.' But why 'Suspended in Gaffa'? Maybe it's that moment when you feel you're falling just as you're dropping off to sleep. Maybe it's 'gaffer tape' that essential tool of roadies and film crews which holds anything and everything together; but written 'Gaffa' to look like a place, like Huxley's 'Eyeless In Gaza'.

In the Garden of Eden we have half of heaven (the answer – Nirvana) but we can't have it all 'unless we can prove that we're doing it.' Doing what? You won't know until you're doing it. It's no good blaming others for your problems – bluffing gets you nowhere in the search for truth. The second verse is based on the words of Christ: You can't remove a splinter from someone's eye while you have a plank in your own. And it is easier for a camel to pass through the eye of a needle (a very small gate to the walled city of Jerusalem) than for a rich man to enter the Kingdom of God. The third verse takes us back to Greek mythology – Pandora was the first woman on Earth and she carried a jar (box) of secrets. When she opened this out flew all the evils that beset the Earth (like the cover of 'Never For Ever'!). Only Hope was left in the box. But I 'won't open boxes I am told not to.' "We had to clear out this old room for her den," remembered a school friend, "and we found a big glass bottle with a stopper. Kate stopped me opening it. She thought evil spirits would come out."

This is Kate's only track to feature her early benefactor Dave Gilmour – on backing vocals. This is odd as she admires his guitar playing, and as they share the same record company there should have been no contractual problems. "I think he's a fantastic guitarist because he doesn't go through this blinding . . . it's real emotions, simple – I think that's what music is really about."

'Leave It Open' is like a primal scream or someone letting demons out – strange voices speaking through a 'babbling mouth' (like in 'The Exorcist'). She used to let all her demons out when she was young until she learnt to keep her mouth shut. But they do more harm when they're bottled up inside, so she learned to let it out. And finally if you leave it open you can let other things in – 'let the weirdness in,' weird is just different, don't fear it.

Weird voices were to become something of a speciality for Kate, starting with this album. Just as her good looks gave her the confidence to experiment with grotesque expressions, so the strength, range and quality of her voice gave her the courage to play tricks with it, shrieking, groaning, babbling and even playing it backwards. It is natural for a singer to act with her voice but Kate decided to go further than this. She uses it like an instrument so it becomes part of the texture of the sound, conveying a mood – anger, fear, confusion, like a sound effect or an atmospheric film score. She does this not only in backing vocals, which might be expected, but even in lead lines, occasionally making them virtually unintelligible.

The lyrics of Kate's songs are very important. They are not merely something to sing about or a trite sentiment invested with meaning by a good singer. They are the expression of a developing philosophy. An understanding of the words is vital to a full appreciation of Kate's work (millions of foreign sales notwithstanding). Kate has solved the problem by insisting that the lyrics are printed on every album.

1980

25th November 1980. Kate appears on Russell Harty's early evening chat show along with Julian Lloyd-Webber and Dr Eric Fenby to talk about the Bradford-born composer Delius. The programme featured a re-run of Kate's song *Delius*, the video for which she had made for the *Dr Hook* TV special a few months earlier.

December 1980. *Woman's World* publish an article written by Kate entitled 'How can you eat dead animals?'
Profiles In Rock TV documentary prepared about Kate. Interviews conducted at East Wickham Farm.

2nd December 1980. *December Will Be Magic Again* makes an early festive onslaught on the airwaves, making number 39 in the charts.

9th December 1980. *December Will Be Magic Again* up 10 places to 29 in the BMRB charts, its highest position, though this didn't mean that the airplay for the single waned up to and through Christmas. Around this time the charts were soon to be heavily disrupted by John Lennon's murder, which physically took the real magic out of this particular Christmas.

10th December 1980. *Babooshka* enters the French charts at number five.

Even stranger perhaps are her backwards vocals. The Beatles were the first (pop) artists to try playing tapes backwards ('Rain' and 'Tomorrow Never Knows' 1966). Bowie took this further on 'Lodger'. He explained how he happened to play an old tape of his backwards and found the sound so fascinating that he learnt to sing the vocals like that and reproduced them on 'Move On'. Only afterwards did he play the tape forwards and found it was 'All The Young Dudes'. Kate has also tried this technique, and Paddy gave an hilarious impression of her backwards singing at the 1985 Fan Club/Homeground convention. (*Homeground* is the principal unofficial but recognised fanzine.)

"The weirdest damn record I've ever heard" is how *Melody Maker*'s Colin Irwin described 'The Dreaming' when it was released as a single. Kate wrote an explanation for the official review copies:

"The Aboriginals are not alone in being pushed out of their land by modern man, by their diseases or for their own strange reasons. It is very sad to think they might all die. 'The Dreaming' is the time for Aboriginals when humans took the form of animals, when spirits were free to roam and in this song as the civilised begin to dominate, the 'original ones' dream of dream-time."

Kate had summoned all her talents to create a tone poem for another continent and another age. She had spent six months in Australia as a child and visited there again on promotional tours. The sound of the song was partly inspired by Rolf Harris's 'Sun Arise', and she was pleased to feature him on digeridu. 'Sun Arise' reached number three in 1962 and was one of her choices on the Paul Gambaccini show. "The digeridu is such a circular sound, it's incredibly rooted in the earth. It does have quite a specific rhythm, that sort of slow spacey thing. It's almost like landscapes, huge deserted flat lands. That's what the music talks about – that's where they live, their environment."

"I think a lot of the ideas on this album have been things I've wanted to do for years but just haven't been ready for or haven't had the time. Because the whole tribal and ethnic thing has been happening within my family because of my brother Paddy for 10 years – he's the one who's been gradually pulling me that way. Even on the first album there were a lot of unusual instruments hidden amongst the arrangements which were speaking from my side of things and my brothers'. And I think gradually each time I've done an album I've got more control and therefore been able to portray a lot more of what I mean to get across."

Again, as in 'Pull Out The Pin', Kate looks through the eyes of a minority at the Western world's smothering of a subculture.

Now she waves her magic wand and with a single dancing phrase of Liam O'Flynn's pipes plucks us back across the world to another threatened culture. 'Night Of The Swallow' was recorded in Dublin with members of Planxty and The Chieftains in July 1981, reaffirming Kate's connections with Ireland and its music. It was released as a single in Eire. No drum-machine here; she is back at the piano. Using cinematic images she shows us a man of the gun about to migrate like a bird and she pleads with him not to leave her. Kate treads carefully in politics but she can feel her way into the subject through the personal angle. She returns to the problem of a woman's loyalty in 'Mother Stands For Comfort'. This track was issued as a single in Eire.

In 'All The Love' Kate uses the Eastern idea that we enjoy life after life to imagine having been given a second chance. But people are so afraid to love or show love that though they waited first time, when she gives them 'all the love' they think she's up to something weird. So she becomes afraid of them and leaves her answerphone to deal with them; the machine is a metaphor for all the barriers we create.

1980

30th-31st December 1980. Kate ends the year by guesting on consecutive evenings on two one-hour radio shows hosted by Paul Gambaccini. Kate chose a mixture of favourite tunes spanning classical and popular interests. Tracks chosen:
Kimiad – Alan Stivell.
Do Me Amma – A.L. Lloyd.
To Be Sung Of A Summer's Night On The Water – Delius.
Meetings With Remarkable Men – (Film soundtrack).
An Speic Seodrack – Gabriel McKeon.
Kyrie Eleison And The Mezzuin – David Fanshawe.
The Handsome Cabin Boy – A.L. Lloyd.
Complaint Pour Saint Catherine – Kate and Anna McGarrigle.
Allegri's Miserere – King's College Choir.
Oh Willow Wailey – Isla Cameron.
Farewell To Eiran – Kevin Burke And The Bothy Band.
Another Day – Roy Harper.
Tropical Hot Dog Night – Captain Beefheart.
Sun Arise – Rolf Harris.
Number 9 Dream – John Lennon.
Quiet Departure – Eberhard Weber.
Lord Of The Reedy River – Donovan.
Babylon Sisters – Steely Dan.
The Smell Of Home – Jules And The Polar Bears.
Montana – Frank Zappa.

Photo: *Madeleine Bell, Joe Brown, Leslie Duncan, Pete Townshend, Kate and the late Phil Lynott recording 'Sing Children Sing' for UNICEF, 1979.*

1981

1st January 1981. Capital Radio listeners vote Kate number one artist for the third year in a row.

Kate takes a few weeks off for a holiday.

4th January 1981. Kate's TV Special repeated on BBC1.

10th January 1981. Telephone interview with Kate published in *Record Mirror*, conducted by Chas De Walley.

21st February 1981. *Sounds* readers' poll declares Kate number one Female Singer for 1980. Similar polls in *Smash Hits*, *Record Mirror* and *Melody Maker* reveal a similar pattern.

Babooshka remains in the French top 30 for nearly two months, slipping at the end of February. The same record stays top 10 in Italy through January and February.

March 1981. Kate works in her 8-track home studio preparing new material.

May 1981. Recording begins on LP *The Dreaming*.

21st June 1981. *Sat In Your Lap/Lord Of The Reedy River* single released. A-side inspired after Kate attended a Stevie Wonder concert in London.

Video for *Sat In Your Lap* made at Abbey Road.

July 1981. Recording continues at Abbey Road studios. Kate also records one track with The Chieftains (*Night Of The Swallow*) on a brief trip to Dublin.

14th July 1981. Kate appears on *Razzamatazz* children's TV show talking about the making of the *Sat In Your Lap* video at Abbey Road studios.

Photo: *Kate and classical violinist Nigel Kennedy at the BPI Awards.*

'Houdini' is about the escape artist "From Mrs Houdini's point of view. His wife was involved with his work and used to help with the tricks. Before he went off into his tank where he was all tied up she would give him a parting kiss and pass him a tiny little key which he used in the water to unlock the chains. And since I heard that imagery I thought it was so beautiful and so extraordinary."

Kate spoke about this song in an interview on Capital Radio. "He was really close to his mother and when she died he needed desperately to try and communicate with her through a medium. So he came across all these people who were making money out of the art of pretending to speak to the dead. When he realised they were ruining people's lives just to make money he decided to show that they were frauds, so he spent years of his life doing this.

"Before he died he said to his wife, 'I'm going to die before you but when I do I'm gonna try everything I can to come back through a real medium. But I'm going to use words that only you and I know – a code so you'll know it's me and no one else.' So they made this code together – 'Rosabel believe' – and when he died she went round all the seances waiting for him to appear. He was escaping chains and then trying to escape death." Not even Eternity can hold Houdini.

"As soon as there was an emotional contact with that woman who was really in love with him it became a perfect angle to write from." Houdini is a powerful image for Kate, who wishes to believe that love is stronger than death. 'You and I Rosabel believe.' "It was really *sad* trying to be Houdini's lady, because he had died and obviously he must have been amazingly special as a person."

If love is to be stronger than death, how great a betrayal is rape. Indeed 'Get Out Of My House!' is so emotional it feels like a betrayal to analyse it. But it needs little analysis. The song shakes with hysteria, panic and anger. The heaviest drum sound is a real slamming door. Kate's house is her body – 'This house is as old as I am' – and soul – 'This house knows all I have done'. You can hear her heart hammering and she stutters in madness – the sound is awash with adrenalin. 'With my key I . . .' Kiyai! is the martial arts cry which reverberates through the body turning panic into anger, fear into fight.

'I face towards the wind, I change into the Mule.' A mule is the offspring of a horse and a donkey and is reputed to be stubborn and always sterile. In Isaac Asimov's great science fiction epic 'The Foundation' the Mule is a mutant who is spurned for his ugliness. But he finds he can read minds and uses this power to become the terrifying ruler of the galaxy. 'Hee-Haw Hee-Haw' – the braying of the Mule is full of ugliness and danger. The album ends with ominous chanting.

"It is quite dark, without meaning to be negative. I think nearly all those songs are saying people are great but they really hurt each other."

'The Dreaming' was released in September and left most of the reviewers puzzled. However in December it peaked in the charts at number three and in due course went gold. Kate's finger was more surely on the pulse than the EMI execs. One critic who wasn't puzzled was the communist daily *The Morning Star* (sounds like a Kate Bush song title!) who said: "Kate Bush's 'The Dreaming' was the most outstanding contribution from any woman artist this year."

THE VIDEO FILE

Photo: *Kate on manoeuvres.*

1981

August 1981. Recording continues at central London's Odyssey studios. Material for the new LP gradually forming.

6th August 1981. Appears on *Looking Good, Feeling Fit* discussing dancing and fitness.

12th November 1981. Abbey Road celebrates 50 years as a recording studio, attended by Kate and many other musicians who had made Abbey Road so special.

21st November 1981. Kate interviewed on BBC2's *Friday Night, Saturday Morning* late night show.

"When I'm performing I do have a very different way of looking from when I'm quite normal."(KB 1979)

When Kate first hit the headlines and television screens the art (and the science) of video was still in its infancy. There had been promotional pop films ever since the early sixties, usually made by American artists to promote their records in Britain and around the States when they were unable to appear in person. *Top Of The Pops*, this country's only TV chart programme at the time, used to feature these rather dull excursions which either showed a patently mimed performance with none of the zap of the real thing or else the star strolling through an unlikely outdoor setting. The most successful of the pre-video film clips were those of (usually black American) artists giving electric live performances. The camera was just there to record an exciting event.

With 18 months training and preparation behind her, Kate should have been ready to burst into video, and in a sense she was. Her interest was not in exploring the medium but in using it as a means of presenting her own performance and the ideas that were burning in her since Lindsay Kemp had opened her eyes. Though very different from the all-singing-all-dancing American entertainers Kate's early videos were in this mould. They didn't trouble with technical effects and possibilities but went straight for performance – nor did they ignore the fact that a very attractive young woman was prepared to pour herself through the camera and onto the screen.

Kate's first appearance on *Top Of The Pops* was an embarrassment and disappointment to her, despite the impact she undoubtedly had on a new generation of fans – "All stiletto heels, exploding hair and theatrical gestures". She sang 'Wuthering Heights' in black top and red slacks, and watching it afterwards realised her mistake – the costume had to match the mood and the message. Thus her first video shows, with startling simplicity, a young woman with wild hair and flowing white robes – looking for all the world like Mr Rochester's poor mad wife in sister Charlotte Brontë's *Jane Eyre*. She is of no time and no place – a ghost radiating light. The swirling mist and mirror floor seem at times to form a watery horizon and she appears in multiple image dancing with grand flowing gestures matching the sweep of the anthem.

71

These are very basic steps for anyone fresh out of dance class but they were entirely new to rock in 1978, as was the total commitment of performance by this strange new star.

This video is not particularly imaginative or innovative but the image of this eager, intense, beautiful figure is exceedingly powerful and belongs better to the song than some literal view of windy moors which could only have distracted from the simple strength of the performance. (The *Monty Python* team demonstrated the dangers of that approach with Cathy and Heathcliff waving semaphore flags!)

The first image in 'Wuthering Heights' is a hazy vertically-reflected shape like a Rorschach test or an Indian goddess suspended in mid screen. The next video, 'The Man With The Child In His Eyes' develops this idea to produce a patch of light-plasma which firms into a floating curled-up embryo while a voice cries, 'He's here! He's here!' As Kate starts singing we see her face in soft focus as she sings with the extreme of shining-eyed passion a teenage girl might share with her mirror. She is wearing a second skin of lurex body-stocking resembling glittering flesh and her lithe arms move like a fledgling trying out its wings. These contract-release gestures are again straight out of a contemporary dance class but she projects a quality which is seldom seen on screen and never in the pop arena.

Some viewers felt challenged and even affronted at being drawn into so intimate a display of emotion. Debbie Harry never came on like this! Such self-exposure was very brave and invited ridicule – and was a godsend to several comedians and impressionists! (Kate actually wrote to Faith Brown thanking her for doing such a brilliant impersonation.) Nonetheless many red-blooded males must have imagined themselves as the man with this child in their eyes. But was that her intention?

1982

January 1982. Recording continues at Advision studios.

May 1982. *The Dreaming* LP now mixed and ready for September release.

June 1982. Completes session work with singer/songwriter Zaine Griff.

21st July 1982. Performs at the Prince's Trust Royal Gala at the Dominion Theatre, London.

27th July 1982. *The Dreaming/Dreamtime* single released. The single reaches number 48 in the charts after minimal airplay.

10th August 1982. Kate interviewed live on Radio 1 about the new LP at Covent Garden's Piazza.

Pictorial Press

There was much early controversy about Kate's promotion as a sex symbol. Photographers soon discovered her openness with the camera and EMI obviously felt they were on to a winner, peddling her appeal for all she was worth. After some criticism of sexploitation Kate rejected some early images but she cannot have been unaware of what was going on. When asked early in 1979 if she encouraged the audience as voyeurs she replied, "I don't know . . . maybe I do. I'm probably quite calculating behind my creativity."

But sex and sexuality has always been an essential ingredient of Kate's writing and it would have been strange had it not carried over into her performance, particularly as she has always been keen to combine every means of expression into a unified whole.

On stage or screen Kate is never afraid to look ridiculous. She is just as ready to contort her face in disgust or fear as to pout her lips and flutter her eyelashes. She is miming these activities, signalling emotions larger than life as part of a stylised theatrical performance.

Julie Angel

'Hammer Horror' with its gargoyle expressions was Kate's next video and represented a big step forward in technique and imagination. Dressed as a Victorian widow, Kate steps into the spotlight and finds herself swept up by a macabre 'executioner/torturer' figure – Anthony van Laast in black mask. Anthony, principal dancer with the London Contemporary Dance Company, helped Kate realise the ideas she had for this number – and for many numbers on the tour which she started planning at this time. He was able to extend her technique far beyond her dance class repertoire and the result is so good that she returned to the idea years later in the marvellous video for 'Running Up That Hill'.

Once again the camera is fairly static and the conception is essentially a filmed performance, theatrical in its music, staging and lighting. What is impressive is that the video is shot in only five long 'takes' requiring continuous flawless performance but resulting in greater intensity. The close-ups allow the black figure to creep up on her (and on us) as if appearing out of nowhere.

'Wow' is about theatre and the sort of people Kate met in Lindsay's company. It is virtually a record of the performance she did on the tour, but without the diversion of the male dancers in their flowing skirts. There is a marvellous effect of Kate floating as she waves her arms – surely she's not actually wearing a harness? The line 'hitting the vaseline' is illustrated with a cheeky pat on the bum which got the video banned from *Top Of The Pops* until she shot an alternative sequence.

On *The Whole Story* there is a different video for 'Wow', a lively series of clips taken (exclusively) from the tour video. This was for two reasons – "Firstly I really don't like the promo we did for 'Wow'. I think it's silly. Also looking through the videos I noticed a great absence of 'performance' promos and the tour was an important part of the story."

'Them Heavy People' came after the tour and showed more confidence. It continued the series of theatrical vignettes but this time Kate gave herself more scope. (She artlessly clambers over the table avoiding the swinging light bulb without apparent contrivance.) The video is unusual in that it uses as its sound track a live recording (the tour EP) but does not pretend to recreate a live show. On tour Kate had appeared with the two boy dancers in trench coats and fedoras as three heavy people – thirties gangsters with Cagney gestures. On stage the male outfit contrasted effectively with the others she wore. But now for the video she dresses more seductively in a marvellous cerise skirt with side splits and a black top with zips over her breasts – set off nicely by the man's fedora. She also wears high-heels – on the tour she was always barefoot.

Kate presents herself as very strong in the stylised fight with the two men, but throughout it all she remains strangely uninvolved with the dancers. This isolation is maintained through all her videos until 'The Hair Of The Hound' set. She is presented as a central figure whose relationship with the camera is never threatened by the ciphers who appear with her.

1982

13th September 1982. *The Dreaming* released.

THE DREAMING (EMI) EMC 3419

Side One
Sat In Your Lap
drums: Preston Heyman
bass: Jimmy Bain
piano, fairlight: Kate Bush
sticks: Paddy Bush, Preston Heyman
backing vocals: Ian Bairnson, Gary Hurst, Stewart Arnold, Paddy Bush
CMI trumpet section: Geoff Downes

There Goes A Tenner
drums: Stuart Elliot
bass: Del Palmer
synclavier: Dave Lawson
piano, fairlight, C.S.80: Kate Bush

Pull Out The Pin
drums: Preston Heyman
string bass: Danny Thompson
piano: Kate Bush
electric guitar: Brian Bath
backing vocals: Dave Gilmour

Suspended In Gaffa
drums and sticks: Stuart Elliot
bass: Del Palmer
piano: Kate Bush
strings: Paddy and Kate Bush
mandolins: Paddy Bush
synclavier: Dave Lawson

Leave It Open
drums: Preston Heyman
bass: Jimmy Bain
electric guitar: Alan Murphy
acoustic guitar: Ian Bairnson
piano, fairlight: Kate Bush

In April 1980 came 'Breathing', the first real video – a concept which could not simply be performed on a stage. On *The Whole Story* this follows 'The Man With The Child In His Eyes' – very effectively as there is a strong foetal image to 'Man', and 'Breathing' presents the startling and powerful image of Kate in a plastic womb with a spiralling umbilical chord. This outsize bubble is obviously artificial but no less effective for that – Kate is learning from pop art how to overlay visual images much as she layers sounds and meanings.

Rocking to and fro, Kate appears to be clothed only in a film of see-through plastic giving a strong sense of eroticism as in nearly all her videos. There is also the suggestion of space suits and capsules – images which David Bowie was to use later that year in his seminal video 'Ashes To Ashes' (which Kate herself referred back to in her video for 'The Dreaming'). The previous year the film 'Alien' had made its extraordinary impact on the imagination and H. R. Giger's organic space-ship design must have struck a chord with Kate in her identification of womb and room, home and body. (He later designed the Cloudbusting machine for her.)

The space theme is reinforced in the instrumental/voice-over section when Kate and the camera roll about to produce an amazingly fluid, zero-gravity effect.

1982

Side Two
The Dreaming
drums: Stuart Elliot
didgeridoo : Rolf Harris
piano, fairlight: Kate Bush
animals: Percy Edwards
bullroarer, backing vocals: Paddy Bush
crowd: Gosfield Goers

Night Of The Swallow
drums: Stuart Elliot
fretless, 8-string bass: Del Palmer
piano, fairlight: Kate Bush
pipes and strings written and arranged:
Bill Whelan
Uillean pipes, penny whistle: Liam O'Flynn
fiddle: Sean Keane
bouzouki: Donnal Lunny

All The Love
drums, percussion: Stuart Elliot
bass: Del Palmer
piano, fairlight: Kate Bush
choirboy: Richard Thornton

Houdini
drums: Stuart Elliot
bass: Eberhard Weber
piano, fairlight: Kate Bush
strings written and arranged: Dave Lawson, Andrew Powell
'Houdini': Gordon Farrell
'Rosabel Believe': Del Palmer

Get Out Of My House
drums: Preston Heyman
bass: Jimmy Bain
electric guitars: Alan Murphy
piano, fairlight: Kate Bush
backing vocals: Paddy Bush
'Eeyore': Paul Hardiman
drum talk: Esmail Sheikh

As white light predominates over the suffused red glow this ill-fated foetus is born/aborted/thrust into the world at the moment of holocaust. Other victims are rendered incandescent by the nuclear explosion, then their silhouettes dissolve to reveal a dead world of polluted water. All the figures are hard-edged and flat like a collage – another effect seen later in 'Ashes To Ashes'. The technical effects in this video are still primitive by today's standards but they are used with such imagination that the images reinforce the power of the anthem.

'Babooshka' by contrast is tremendous fun. Kate uses a double-bass to great effect, miming the strong bass line of the music and playing with the sensual shape of the instrument. She wears a veil, suggesting both age and beauty hidden beneath, then whips it off (with smart cutting) to produce a transformation into what must surely be her most provocative outfit.

Unfortunately a strike on BBC TV meant that 'Babooshka' was hardly seen at the time of its release but the following January at the first Midem Video Awards Kate won the award for Best International Performance while Keef Macmillan won the Best International Production Award.

'Army Dreamers' takes us out on location with Kate throwing herself into action as a soldier with a KT (Bush Band) arm-band. The video opens with a close-up of a mascara-rimmed eye blinking each time the rifle bolt clicks home. This is a true video device which could not be done on stage. (Eyes and masks seem to be a theme in these videos – 'Hammer Horror', 'Sat In Your Lap', 'Running Up That Hill', 'Experiment IV'.) The camera draws back to show a surreal mixture of lipstick and camouflage. As the army unit stalks through the forest their real movements are stylized to produce the effect of dance, another advance in Kate's use of choreography. Again this is a simple video with effective images – the gun changing to a guitar, the little boy growing up shot by shot, the beauty and horror of a body flying through the air from an explosion.

Left: *Dave Gilmour, Kate and Peter Gabriel performing at the 1987 Amnesty International concert.*

This was the last video which Keef Macmillan directed for Kate. He directed all the early videos and the Tour Of Life. Probably as with Andrew Powell she felt it was time to move on. Although these early videos now appear rather tame in their use of the medium Keef was probably a good collaborator for Kate, allowing her space for complete free expression. A more 'tricksy' director might have left us a poorer record of her developing performance.

'Sat In Your Lap' is a curious piece. It was shot in EMI's number one studio at Abbey Road, the big studio used for film music, which has a distinctive polished wood parquet floor like a skating rink. Kate wears a white ballet tutu and has an odd page-boy hair style with a fringe.

The song is about the difficulties of acquiring knowledge and the fools' and dunces' costumes are plain enough. (The Fool was the traditional court jester who played the fool but had to be very clever in his wit – his costume was the quartered colours and hat with points). Some people see overtones of Ku Klux Klan in the white outfits but surely these are simply white costumes to match the tall white dunces caps (which erring school children had to wear, standing in disgrace in a corner of the classroom). The horned devils are minotaurs, mythical monsters with the head of a bull and the body of a man.

The whole charade is lively if not particularly deep, with funny touches like the flying book and tiny figures dancing in the corner of the screen. The clapperboard says '17/6/85 Take 5', the date of filming. Once again we get a close-up of an eye, this time with Kate seeing herself 'in her mind's eye'. She produces a new expression of indignant scorn for 'just when I think I'm king'. But what does it all mean?

This video and 'Suspended In Gaffa' were directed by Brian Wiseman. In both of these the camera is still basically 'stage front' but does rise and fall effectively.

'The Dreaming' marks another step forward in Kate's accomplishment in the medium –and maybe in the budget as well! (Paul Henry directed this and 'Tenner'.) She obviously felt a great challenge and responsibility to do justice to her theme. The action takes place on a remarkable set (created in a large video studio in Wandsworth) representing the ancient Australian landscape and looking rather like the Moon. Kate spins in space (as in the 'Gaffa' video) before landing in the primeval earth. Then she moves off in a series of wonderful kangaroo hops – the kangaroo hops on its toes using its massive tail as a counterbalance.

1982

Produced by: Kate Bush
Recorded: Advision and Odyssey Studios
Engineer: Paul Hardiman
Assistant engineers: David Taylor, Teri Reed
Abbey Road Studios
Engineer: Haydn Bendall
Assistant engineers: Danny Dawson, John Barrett
Townhouse Studios
Engineers: Nick Launay, Hugh Padgham
Assistant engineers: Howard Gray, George Chambers, Nick Cook
All mixes engineered by Paul Hardiman at Advision Studios
Assistant engineer: David Taylor
Digital editing: Peter Woolliscroft
Cut: Ian Cooper
Songs written and arranged: Kate Bush
Photos and toning: Kindlight
Aquatinting: Nick Price
Sleeve co-ordination: Bill Clark
Kate's sleeve notes: "Many thanks to: Graham Middleton, Jim Jones, Mike King, Steve Payne, Step Lang, Duncan Mackay, Kay Hunter, Bob Parr and Brian Tench at Mayfair Studios, David Woolley and Nigel Barker at AIR Studios, Chris Gibbons at Odyssey Studios and all at Advision and Abbey Road Studios. Special thanks to: Del Palmer, Jay, Paddy, Ma & Pa, Lisa, Hil, Andrew, Paul Hardiman, Dave Gilmour, Bill Whelan, Alan Murphy, Haydn and Dan Dan the Suchi man, Jon Kelly and to everyone who has helped to complete and inspire this album."

The dancers are Aboriginals, coming to life out of the land as trees and rocks according to legend. They are wearing curious space-suit costumes which are both modern and primitive in their organic appearance.

There is a strong sense of ritual in the movements and dance – though the hitch-hiker motif is an odd touch! Kate uses reverse shooting (running the film backwards) for an effective shot of smoke being sucked sharply into her mouth (this device is later used again in 'Experiment IV'). We also see a laser line of light (life force?) being pulled out of the stomach of a dying Aborigine. The story ends starkly but vividly with the bodies sinking back into the ground muttering words through the sand.

'Suspended In Gaffa' gives us another unusual setting in a derelict mill. The dust on the floor is very effective and while not a true video effect is certainly something which would be difficult to enact on stage. Kate wears a curious costume – a quilted tunic almost like a uniform. She does a lovely mime of holding a fluttering bird in her hands – similar again to some Bowie moves (which is not to suggest either copied the other). Kate's mother appears at one point to comfort her – the first time any woman has appeared in a Kate Bush video. There is a clever piece of cutting when Kate sucks her thumb and turns into a baby, then a foetus floating on a cloud like 'The Man With The Child In His Eyes'. Later another smooth cut has Kate and the camera tumbling into space (for those of us still wondering what or where Gaffa is). At the end there is the wonderful theatrical device where she disappears into thin air – produced by clever use of light and shadow, not by a simple video dissolve.

In 'There Goes A Tenner' Kate tries her first real story video, a pointer towards her later work. This is in no way filmed theatre, it is conceived in its own medium. Again as in 'Army Dreamers' she does not abandon dance but uses the natural movements of the situation as a basis for choreography, giving the piece a dreamlike mood. We see the burglars creeping about and . . . "One of the bits of the song is all about waiting – the first time they're waiting for something to go wrong and the second time they're waiting for the guy to blow the safe up. The dance routine is based on waiting. The rest of the dance is more or less acting out what the story is." This sense of time hanging over them is emphasised by the wonderful device of a huge pendulum like Edgar Allan Poe's short story *The Pit And The Pendulum*. There is a witty use of blue-screen (superimposition) technique when a blind is pulled down to reveal Del as the driver waiting outside.

'There Goes A Tenner' failed to make the radio playlists and the video was hardly seen. The single failed even to chart. Nearly three years of silence followed which made the release of *The Singles File* video a particularly welcome Christmas treat for deprived fans. For two weeks in February 1984 this became the best selling music video in the UK. Three years later it was superseded by the release of *The Whole Story* which included the video 'EP' 'Hair Of The Hound' and the new 'Experiment IV'. Exclusive to *The Singles File* are 'Hammer Horror', the original 'Wow', 'Suspended In Gaffa' and 'There Goes A Tenner'. The first two are actually better performed on the tour video but 'Gaffa' and 'Tenner' are well worth seeing.

It is interesting to follow how Kate's ideas have developed. From the first her writing was extraordinarily mature but she took time to realise the potential of video, unlike Bowie who was quick to grasp the possibilities of the medium but slower in developing real songwriting maturity. He also worked with Lindsay Kemp and experimented in combining mime with film. In an early piece, 'The Mask', filmed by Ken Pitt (on 'Love You Till Tuesday') he enacts a story against a white background, using sound effects to replace scenery. It was always his way to play with a medium – "I can never leave sources alone!"

At this time Kate was concentrating more on the personal changes her contact with Lindsay had produced. Her experiments were in performance itself and she was keen to have the camera record what she was projecting – she looked and sounded unique and that was enough. Video literacy was low at this time and most viewers were simply bowled over by this new experience.

As the medium developed and budgets increased Kate felt no need to pile on the glamour. Most pop videos rely on girls and cars and the presentation of ostentatious wealth but she had no inclination to spend money on fabulous clothes and looking like a star. Unlike some rags-to-riches artists she had never known want and her ambition was simply to further the creative process. She was similarly unconcerned about looking beautiful. When it comes to appearance, the play's the thing, and she is as likely to play Lady Macbeth as Cleopatra. When Kate portrays a man-killer she reaches for her gun before her lipstick.

1982

LP reviews were mixed, often confused as to its real meaning. Neil Tennant, then of *Smash Hits* magazine, now of The Pet Shop Boys wrote:

"Very weird. Obviously she's trying to become less accessible. Even so this has a haunting atmosphere." (*Smash Hits* 11/11/82.)

14th September 1982. Kate signs copies of *The Dreaming* at London's Virgin Megastore.

Appears on *The Old Grey Whistle Test* for an interview with Mark Ellen and David Hepworth.

21st September 1982. Appears on *Razzamatazz* to perform new single *There Goes A Tenner*.

LP promotion continues in Germany, Spain and Italy. Kate performs *The Dreaming* on TV and conducts radio, press and TV interviews.

2nd October 1982. Kate interviewed on BBC's *Saturday Superstore* by DJ Mike Read.

6th October 1982. Kate travels to Glasgow to continue LP promotion. Attends a party for regional record dealers.

7th October 1982. PA in Newcastle.

8th October 1982. PA in Birmingham.

Interview with Paul Gambaccini for BBC's *Pebble Mill At One* (broadcast October 29th).

Kate interviewed in all the major music papers and magazines.

28th October 1982. Sixty-minute interview with Kate broadcast on France-Inter.

HOUNDS OF LOVE

LFI

"If it had been possible for Kate to do that eight years ago she would have done."(Alan Murphy, guitar.)

It began in the early seventies – the new super-groups looking for the ultimate super-studio. It was a bit like in-crowd clubs – just as everyone discovers the most popular place the whisper passes and the elite move on to a new paradise. The equipment became more and more fabulous, and this is not just fashion of course, these are the hi-tech tools of the job. Even the locations became more sun-drenched and exotic – Chateau d'Herouville, Jamaica, Nassau, Montserrat. But Kate was always more concerned with the work in hand than the scene outside and mostly preferred to work in London, near to home. It was obvious where her dream studio would be situated – right in her back garden.

When Kate was a child she and her brothers used to play and practise in the old barns behind the farmhouse. One of the first things she did with her EMI advance money was to equip one of the barns as a rehearsal room. She and Paddy installed a piano and later an 8-track recorder so she could try out new ideas and get them down while they were fresh in her mind. Then she was able to transfer them to the big tapes in professional studios so none of that original spirit would be lost. Now Kate had one more step to take in this process – the biggest step.

"Working in commercial studios was something I couldn't continue to do. The way I work is very experimental and when you're in a studio that's costing a phenomenal amount of money every hour it puts too much pressure on you. It just zaps any creativity – you feel too oppressed to create properly. So we wanted to build and equip our own recording studio which was quite a big commitment but one of the best decisions I've made." The old barn was to become a professional 24-track studio. Work began in June 1983. Once again the family rallied round.

As usual Kate spent the rest of the year after the release of her last LP in promotion. In September she started preliminary work on the new LP in commercial studios as the home-base was still in preparation. At Christmas her first collection of promotional videos, *The Singles File*, was released followed by 'The Singles File' box set of records. EMI were doing what they could to bridge the lengthening gap between LPs.

1982

November 1982 (Early). LP promotions continue in Germany.
Suspended In Gaffa single released except in the UK.

2nd November 1982. *There Goes A Tenner/Ne T'Enfuis Pas* single released in the UK.

13th November 1982. *The Dreaming* released in the USA.

1983. Kate finally finds the real route for her career. Pressures to tour are forgotten so that she can concentrate on her first love, recording. Notable chronological dates become few and far between as more and more time is spent in the studio.

77

In the five years since 'Wuthering Heights' and 'The Kick Inside' first hit the charts she had made three LPs and undertaken one tour. To most pop people this would have been an easy ride. But Kate is such a relentless pursuer of creative goals that her time had been very fully used and in reality she had hardly taken a break. "So I did this, taking in new stimulus so the new material wouldn't be of the same energy as the last album but would be fresh and interesting."

Kate was very fit in mind and body when she went into the new studio. "I do very much enjoy writing the songs and for me more and more the whole recording-production process is all part of the writing. What I'm doing is actually writing it on to tape so the production, the arrangements, the lyrics, everything are a part of that. It would feel like I wasn't fulfilling the whole process now if I wasn't involved in these areas."

1983

March 1983. Kate nominated for two Ivor Novello Awards by the British Academy of Songwriters.

15th June 1983. Mini LP released in America featuring five tracks.
Work begins on the building of Kate's own 24-track recording studio. Much of the construction overseen by Dr Bush.

July 1983. *Ne T'Enfuis Pas/Un Baiser D'Enfant* single released in French-speaking territories.

September 1983. Work begins on the next LP, *Hounds of Love*. The record would take almost two years to complete.

21st November 1983. *Night Of The Swallow* single released in Ireland.

December 1983. *The Singles File* collection of Kate's video work to-date released in time for the Christmas market. Kate promotes the product with some personal appearances in London.

1984

January 1984. Work begins in earnest on the new LP. Kate utilises the custom-made studio at home. No new material would be released this year.

16th January 1984. Takes time out from recording to open UK's SKY satellite TV station in central London.

23rd January 1984. *The Singles File* boxed set released, a collection of Kate's singles to-date.

'Hounds Of Love' was the extraordinary album created in the new studio and 'Running Up That Hill' the first single, but perhaps the B-side is really the song that christened it. 'Under The Ivy' we did in our studio in just one afternoon." It is easy to imagine Kate at the piano reflecting on the changes wrought since those summers when she used to play in this mouse-infested barn as a child. The simple style harks right back to her earliest compositions. 'This little girl inside me is retreating to her favourite place.' She may smile at the line 'I sit here in the thunder' – the thunder-box was an old-fashioned privy or lavatory, one of the farm's more humble outbuildings.

In August 1985 'Running Up That Hill' burst upon the pop scene and took the country by storm. Gathering fans like the Pied Piper, Kate stormed to number three with her biggest hit since 'Wuthering Heights'. She appeared on *Top Of The Pops* with a large band beating out the relentless rhythm and drew an arrow aimed straight for the heart.

In September the album was released and a week later entered the chart at number one. In due course it went double platinum.

The cover shows Kate swaddled in a pink dream, her hair swirling in a mauve miasma which might be mist, water or shot silk. Her face is a pink mask of transluscent make-up from which her eyes gaze with a dull incurious stare which might be narcotic, post-coital or contemptuously regal. She is embracing two hounds which are even more somnolent. This is both peaceful and disturbing. The back sleeve is a second 'cover' entitled 'The Ninth Wave' as the album is really two projects – two mini-albums.

Throughout Kate Bush's work two themes have preoccupied her – surrendering to love (being lost in love) and being cut off from the world (lost without love). These are two complementary kinds of extinction, two sides of the coin – the two sides of her fifth album 'Hounds Of Love'.

"The last album was dealing with a lot of very different things and very different places, different atmospheres in tracks next to each other. I think there's more a sense of a theme on this album – obviously on the second side but even on the first side. Although they're separate songs I think they have a flavour that's consistent. There's more sense of flow from track to track. I was very happy with the last album. It was certainly a mark for us!" The theme of the first side is unconditional love, from lover or mother, a love which closes around you, to protect or to suffocate.

'It doesn't hurt me!' Liar! We are plunged straight into the relentless beat of obsession. At 108 b.p.m. 'Running Up That Hill' is the nearest Kate has come to disco, though not, we may be sure, for commercial reasons. Disco music with its relentless beat, its unending obsession with love/sex and its sense-surround drug-like pursual of mindless oblivion is just the vehicle for Kate's reluctant plunge into the surrender of love. This is what she believes – fears? – may be the answer to alienation and the terror of being shut out from life.

Buddhists believe that all divisions are false – the universe is one and we are all a part of it. All objects, all creatures, all people are manifestations of one spirit. It is our desires and our mistaken intellect which prevents us accepting that we are not separate. But Kate was not only introduced to Buddhism – she had a big dose of paganism added to the homebrew. So while in early songs ('Symphony In Blue') she was ready to consider that she is part of the universe and that love is a dangerous emotion, over the years she has come to feel that the universe (without love) is cold and lifeless, and that only the fire of love will enable her to fuse with another person and so end her soul's lonely separation . . . Ah, but is that the answer? Can two souls ever know one another? ('Running Up That Hill'.) Or is love the greatest trap of all? ('Hounds Of Love'.)

Love is the greatest test. It is trust versus power-game. "The power of the relationship is something that gets in the way – creates insecurities." So in love you feel your love is so strong that you can never be loved as much in return. Love is complicated and becomes circular – 'Babooshka', where the wife is loved for herself and yet not. "If the man could be the woman and the woman the man, if they could make a deal with God to change places, they'd understand what it's like to be the other person."

Julie Angel

Above: *Rowan Atkinson and Kate sing 'Do Bears' at the Secret Policeman's Ball.*

Strangely, 'Running Up That Hill' never runs, but 'Hounds Of Love' does. Here we finally see the child 'running in the night, afraid of what might be' – the 'child' who wrote the early songs. 'I've always been a coward' – but she is not any longer: 'Here I go! But I'm still afraid to be there among your hounds of love.' (Courage is not the absence of fear but the overcoming of it.) Then that old cry – 'Don't let me go!' The anguish and the ecstasy – 'I need love love love love!'

But it's not all anguish. 'The Big Sky' is a joyous, funny, crazy celebration of life and the world. She is not puzzling over philosophy here, she is celebrating with an affirmation of joy. Maybe love has released her spirit – unlike the people who look down at the ground missing, who never understood her – the journalists who thought she was too wide-eyed, too Gosh! and Golly! Too *Wow!*

'Mother Stands For Comfort' takes us back to anxiety – the fear that made you do something terrible, that makes you want to return to the womb and unconditional love, the first love that didn't tear you apart. "It's dealing with a son who's committed a bad crime and to (his mother) her instincts overrule what's right and wrong. I think that's interesting – how some mothers will overrule their sense of morality because they love their son so much." This song picks up the thread of 'Night Of The Swallow' and even 'James And The Cold Gun'. To her I am 'the hunted not the hunter.'

'I still dream of Organon.' The serene voice soars above a low string quartet.

'Cloudbusting' tells a story again, a true one, but told in a dreamlike, magical way. "I found a book nearly 10 years ago now. I didn't know anything about the writer, I just pulled it off the shelf – it looked interesting. And it was an incredible story. It's written by Peter Reich and it's called *A Book Of Dreams*. It's looking at his father and their relationship through his eyes as a child. It's very emotive and very innocent. His father (Wilhelm Reich) was a respected psychoanalyst, and besides this he made machines called cloudbusters that could make it rain. He and his father used to go out together and make it rain – they used to go cloudbusting." 'Organon' was the name Wilhelm Reich gave to a stretch of land he owned. "Unfortunately the peak in the book is where his father is arrested and taken away from him. He was considered a threat and so suddenly his father is gone. It's a very sad book as well."

Side one, 'Hounds Of Love', explored Kate's ambivalent attitude to love as an answer to the existential problem of isolation and 'that feeling of meaninglessness' ('Symphony In Blue'). 'The Ninth Wave' plunges into the alternative. With tremendous courage she is probing her greatest fascination, her greatest fear. "It was really the concept side that came first. For a good few years I've wanted to play with a piece of music that was more involved than three to five minutes. I was worried that it wouldn't work and until I'd written four or five songs I wouldn't know if it was going to be successful. So I thought it was wise to use just one side of the album and the other side to balance with five or six completely different songs not linked in any way which were more positive and up tempo.

"A lot of people think that the whole side was inspired by a Tennyson poem but finding this quote, looking for a title for the whole thing, was the last piece in a jigsaw."

The cover photo for 'The Ninth Wave' (taken by Kate's brother Jay) is Ophelia in a life-jacket – a young woman floating in water, strewn with wild plants and with her hair flowing about her. This was inspired by a celebrated pre-Raphaelite painting by John Everett Millais.

Ophelia was in love with Hamlet, who pretended to be mad and spurn her love. In her despair Ophelia was herself driven mad – she solemnly gave people flowers with strange messages. At last she fell into a stream and drowned among her flowers, not trying to save herself. Bearing the picture in mind we may draw a few analogies, perhaps not least that Ophelia was very close to her brother (who finally kills Hamlet to avenge her death).

But Kate is not retelling Ophelia's story – this is not another 'Wuthering Heights'. She has her own story to tell. "It's an idea I got a few years ago of someone being in the water

---

Photos: *Wilhelm Reich with baby Peter and Peter Reich as author.*

1985

June 1985. The *Hounds Of Love* LP completed, Kate's fifth LP with EMI.

August 1985. *Running Up That Hill (A Deal With God)/Under The Ivy* single released.

Appears on *Wogan* complete with bow and arrow performing *Running Up That Hill*. The single is a big success in the UK and worldwide and becomes Kate's biggest hit single since *Wuthering Heights*.

22nd August 1985. Performs *Running Up That Hill* on *Top Of The Pops*.

30th August 1985. Appears at the Berlin Music Festival. Performs *Running Up That Hill* and *Cloudbusting* on the West Berlin 8 O'Clock Show.

9th September 1985. The *Hounds Of Love* LP previewed at the London Planetarium where the whole LP was played for press, complemented by a spectacular Laserium laser show production.

16th September 1985. The *Hounds Of Love* LP released in the UK.

HOUNDS OF LOVE (EMI) KAB 1

Side One
**Running Up That Hill
(A Deal With God)**
drums: Stuart Elliot
bass: Del Palmer
guitar: Alan Murphy
balalaika: Paddy Bush

Hounds Of Love
drums: Charlie Morgan, Stuart Elliot
cello: Jonathan Williams

The Big Sky
drums: Charlie Morgan
bass: Youth
guitars: Alan Murphy
didgeridoo: Paddy Bush
percussion: Morris Pert
handclapping: Charlie and Del

Mother Stands For Comfort
drums: Stuart Elliot
bass: Eberhard Weber

Cloudbusting
drums: Stuart Elliot
strings: The Medicci Sextet
arranged for strings: Dave Lawson
backing vocals: Brian Bath, Paddy Bush, John Carder Bush, Del Palmer

for the night. It's hard to say where it came from. I can only pinpoint certain war films like 'The Cruel Sea' where people have been cast into the water having been through quite a heavy experience already. Launching from that is the basis of the body in the water but then the head travels off as the night goes on."

Throughout this song-cycle the ancient and modern are constantly overlaid – helicopters and inquisitors, astronauts and witches. Dreaming has often been an element in Kate's work and here she explores it as far as hallucination and death. She is both exploring the depths of dream and presenting the story like a succession of dreams linked by that loose dream-logic.

'And Dream Of Sheep'

The work opens with a lonely voice accompanied by just a piano. The 'Little Light' is love and life and it lights up her face. ('There's light in love you see' – 'Kashka From Baghdad'.) But it is only a little light. "The song is about someone in the water alone and frightened and they want to go to sleep to get away from the situation but it's dangerous to go to sleep, you could drown." 'White horses' and 'a buoy' are sea images but they carry overtones of sex. She wants to be weak, to sleep and dream of sheep – sheep here are also an image of people who follow blindly without struggling (Gurdjieff's sleepers). This is the supreme temptation – to give up the fight and succumb to death. She will wake to any sound of engines – but left alone she will drown. 'Suspended in Gaffa.'

"When I was little and I'd had a bad dream I'd go into my parents' bedroom round to my mother's side of the bed . . . I'd say 'I've had a bad dream' and she'd lift up the bedclothes and say something like, 'Come here with me now.' It's my mother saying this line in the track." It represents 'motherly comfort'.

The radio with its friendly voices talking about stupid things is to dull her thoughts, blank her troubled imagination – in life, not only in the water and the story. Sheep, sleep, poppies – drugs, all ways of switching off and surrendering.

Some people believe 'The Ninth Wave' is all about drugs. There are certainly drug images here. After poppies we get 'ice', 'white', 'cutting out little lines', 'snow'. Whether or not Kate has ever explored these diversions, she cannot have been in the music business for years without seeing a lot of drug-taking at fairly close hand. But this story is not only about drugs. It deals with a greater existential struggle, though one in which drugs often play a serious role.

'Under Ice'

Sinister chugging cellos break through the thrall of sleep. It's wonderful! – the river has frozen over, she has numbed her pain. She is skating on a mirror, exhilarated. But the ice is splitting and she sees someone under the ice – 'It's me'. This is the terrifying image of Houdini, who was trapped under the ice when one of his escapes went wrong. (Just as he thought he was dying he heard his dead mother calling to him and her voice led him to a hole in the ice.) It is also a kind of 'Through The Looking Glass' as each song, each episode takes us deeper into the soul. 'It's me!' echoes the anguished cry of caged fear at the end of 'Leave It Open' and gives way to the eerie harmonics which ended 'The Infant Kiss'.

1985

Side Two
The Ninth Wave

And Dream Of Sheep
bouzouki: Donal Lunny
whistles: John Sheahan

Under Ice
harmonic vocals: Paddy Bush

Waking The Witch
drums: Charlie Morgan
fairlight bass: Del Palmer
guitars: Alan Murphy
synthesiser sequences: Kevin McAlea
helicopter by kind permission of Pink Floyd *The Wall*

Watching You Without Me
drums: Stuart Elliot
double bass: Danny Thompson

Jig Of Life
drums: Stuart Elliot, Charlie Morgan
fiddles, whistles: John Sheahan
bouzouki, bodhran: Donal Lunny
Uillean pipes: Liam O'Flynn
bass: Del Palmer
didgeridoo: Paddy Bush
narration: John Carder Bush

Hello Earth
drums: Stuart Elliot
bass: Eberhard Weber
guitar: Brian Bath
Uillean pipes: Liam O'Flynn
bouzouki: Donal Lunny
choir: The Richard Hickox Singers, directed by Richard Hickox, arranged for voices by Michael Berkeley

The Morning Fog
guitar: John Williams
bass: Del Palmer
violins, fujare: Paddy Bush
synthesiser: Kevin McAlea

Photo: *Dave Gilmour and Kate perform 'Running Up That Hill' for Amnesty.*

'Waking The Witch'

Voices are trying to wake her, friendly at first – while she regresses into childhood and further back through previous lives (the voices are of different accents and nationalities) until the voices become a mediaeval chant and her mother announces: 'Look who's here to see you!' Then she wakes to the nightmare of an Inquisition as her own speech becomes incoherent, chattering with fear perhaps and unable to defend herself. It could also be the sound of speech breaking in bubbles as they reach the surface.

We hear a nursery/folk chant about posies (Ophelia again) and the ringing of Gothic bells. There is a blackbird being drowned – in their superstition people used to put animals to death thinking they embodied the spirits of witches. The voice of the inquisitor is like that of the devil snarling accusations. As she is found guilty a helicopter breaks into her consciousness with a megaphone shouting 'get out of the waves – get out of the water!'

1985

Written and produced by: Kate
Voices, fairlight, piano: Kate Bush
Engineered by: Del Palmer, Haydn Bendall, Brian Tench, Paul Hardiman, Nigel Walker, James Guthrie
Engineer at Windmill Lane: Bill Somerville-Large
Assistant engineer: Pearce Dunne
Mixed by: Brian Tench
except *Hounds Of Love, Mother Stands For Comfort* mixed by Julian Mendelsohn
All Irish arrangements by Bill Whelan
Orchestral arrangements by Michael Kamen
Jig Of Life: original music discovered by Paddy Bush
Studio maintenance: Jim Jones
Cut by: Ian Cooper
All Linn programming: Del Palmer

Kate's sleeve notes: "Many thanks to all at Abbey Road Studios
Photography: John Carder Bush (Hair – Anthony Yacomine, Make-up – Clayton Howard)
A big woof to Bonnie and Clyde
Design: Bill Smith Studio
Special thanks to Del, Ma and Pa, Jay, Paddy, Melanie, Andrew, Hil, Hay-Ho, Al, Brian, Ken Townsend, Eberhard Weber, Florian Fricke, Werner Herzog, Robbie Coltrane, David Munns, Chris Blair, Vivienne and Dyane.
Thanks to Bill and Denise Whelan, Liam, Donal, John Sheahan, Paddy Glackin, Gabi Zangerl, Madame Maria Nanky, Terry Gilliam, Peter Swallow, Basil and the Young Ones, and a big thank you to Peter Reich.''

Express Newspapers

Julie Angel

'Watching You Without Me'

The next dream/song proceeds with a mood of unnatural calm. She is a ghost in her own home, out of her body and unable to speak to a living person. "When I was little my mother fainted for no apparent reason. My father was there and put her on the bed, but he couldn't feel any pulse so he started doing artificial respiration and so on to revive her. Meanwhile, according to my mum, she'd taken off like a balloon and hit the ceiling. She was looking down from there . . . and calling out 'Leave me alone, I'm all right!' Then I walked in asking 'Where's my mum?' and when she saw me she dropped back down into her body, she says; anyway she did come back to life.'' (Kate also wrote about this, more facetiously, in 'Blow Away'.)

But Ophelia is not surfacing yet. We hear the sea again and her chattering voice interrupts before she says 'You won't hear me leaving.' This is the deepest moment, closest to death.

'Jig Of Life'

At this depth she comes face to face with herself as an old lady, exhorting the girl not to die – 'Never say goodbye to my part of your life – this moment in time doesn't belong to you. C'mon let me live, girl.' She makes the decision – 'I put this moment here.' Then the friendly voice of her brother says 'Over here!' and launches into an Irish chant, the Jig Of Life. 'You will dance in the sunlit pools!'

'Hello Earth'

Returning to life is not easy. Suddenly we are back in the modern world with astronauts, signifying a great distance from Earth, but this time with more control and choices. She is in her car on Earth and looks up to see herself – something bright travelling fast – the little light is shining more brightly now. Then she is looking down on the world watching storms – the storm which first precipitated her into the sea, perhaps. 'I was there at the birth, out of the cloud burst the head of the Tempest, Murderer of calm' – the killer storm again? 'Why did I go?' she asks, and we hear what might be a religious chant of disembodied voices.

'The Morning Fog'

And now she is back, like Scrooge after his spiritual visitations, loving you better now. She is back with her mother, her father, her loved one, her brothers. The end of the song – and of this momentous album – is abrupt and inconsequential, as if cut off. As arbitrary as waking from a dream.

Three further singles were released from this album, 'Cloudbusting' in October, then 'Hounds Of Love' and 'The Big Sky' early in 1986. None did as well as 'Running Up That Hill' and in the USA they barely charted.

Most of the tracks to emerge from the East Wickham studio are more obviously drum-based than before, a trend which started on 'Sat In Your Lap'. In an interview with Tony Myatt recorded for the 1986 Fan Club Convention Kate said, "I think the development of rhythm in my music is perhaps one of the things that makes it obviously more available to people, and a constancy of rhythm wasn't always there on previous albums. I think a very big influence was Del Palmer . . . When I was initially coming up with the songs I would get Del to manifest in the rhythm box the pattern that I wanted. As a bass player he has a natural understanding of rhythms and working with drums and he could also get the patterns I could hear in my head and that I wanted, so it's through him we started off with the rhythmic bass."

Autumn brought 'The Whole Story' and a new single, 'Experiment IV' – a final Hound or a taste of the next album? The Men from the Ministry are even more sinister now, perverting Kate's most personal weapon – her music. "I think music is a very powerful thing and I think it really does affect people." She has always been conscious of the responsibility attached to her gifts and questions the fad which values the opinions of pop stars above those of doctors.

'Experiment IV' also sharply juxtaposes the themes of 'Hounds Of Love'/'The Ninth Wave'. She likens 'a sound that would kill' to falling in love. 'It could feel so bad but it could feel so good' – the fear and ambivalence of 'Running Up That Hill' and 'Hounds Of Love'. 'It could sing you to sleep but that dream is your enemy' – 'And Dream Of Sheep' and the whole of 'The Ninth Wave'.

So what will the next album bring? More profound and anguished struggles with love and death? Or a growing understanding and acceptance of life? She has not solved the riddle – maybe there is no solution and life is about the courage and imagination we summon in confronting the human condition.

© Jamie F. Amos

THE NINTH HOUND
THE NINTH WAVE

1985

20th September 1985. The *Hounds Of Love* LP makes the number one LP position in the first week of release.

September 1985 (Late). Actor Donald Sutherland agrees to appear in Kate's new video for the next single *Cloudbusting*. The video, made in and around Uffington Castle in Oxfordshire, featured Kate as the son of Donald Sutherland, inventor of the Cloudbuster machine (taken from an original story by Peter Reich). The Cloudbuster machine was designed for the video by *Alien* film designer H.R. Giger.

4th October 1985. *Cloudbusting/Burning Bridges* single released.

17th November 1985. LP promotion continues with a trip to New York. As well as personal appearances, Kate also does a number of radio and TV interviews.

November 1985 (Late). TV and radio promotions in France and Germany.

30th November 1985. The official Kate Bush fan club and officially recognised *Homeground* fanzine organise a joint convention in Romford, Essex.

Left: *Painting by Jamie F. Amos — oil on canvas 18″ x 24″.*

HAIR OF THE HOUND

Pictorial Press

1986

10th February 1986. Kate appears live at the BPI Awards in London performing *Hounds Of Love*.

17th February 1986. *Hounds Of Love/The Handsome Cabin Boy* single released in the UK.

February 1986. Peter Gabriel invites Kate to record duet for his next LP *So*. The track, *Don't Give Up* is later released as a single. Kate records her vocal twice on separate visits to Gabriel's studio in Bath.

February 1986 (Late). Kate begins preparation for new video, *The Big Sky*.

6th March 1986. Performs *Hounds Of Love* on *Top Of The Pops*.

March 1986. Kate records appearance for the *Tube's* 100th programme, performing a live version of *Under The Ivy*.

19th March 1986. First day of shooting for Kate's next video of single *The Big Sky*. Members of Kate's fan club featured as enthusiastic audience at the Elstree production.

4th-6th April 1986. Appears alongside Rowan Atkinson at the Comic Relief charity shows in London. Also performs *Breathing* on the same bill.

May 1986. *The Big Sky/Not This Time* single released.

"When we do videos I don't really feel right unless we're all filthy and exhausted by the end of the day."

The leap in style and command which marked the gap between 'The Dreaming' and 'Hounds Of Love' was matched by Kate's next video collection. In different ways these are all conceived as videos – even as mini-films. "I started approaching film directors – I believed that people who make videos would be less likely to make a pop 'video' look like a piece of film. Apart from 'Running Up That Hill' which was edited totally in the video suite, the others were edited on film as much as possible except some special effects. Video is advancing all the time but for me you can't beat the original quality of film."

The quality of these films shows tremendous development in Kate's talents as dancer and actress and marks her début as director. They are immediately set apart from Kate's earlier videos (and from most pop videos) by eliminating the need to 'lip synch' – mime as if singing the song. "As soon as a performer is visually 'singing' they become that performer doing other things while singing. People acting without the lip distractions have more chance of playing a character."

'Running Up That Hill' (directed by David Garfath) is a superb blend of dance and video, the cutting and camera-work being an intrinsic part of the conception. The idea of a dancer being thrown about – possessed – by another dancer first came to Kate for 'Hammer Horror' and here it is developed not merely by technique but by a different kind of commitment from Kate to her partner (Michael Hervieu). For the first time on screen she is appearing, not as the subject of a promotion but as an element in the drama.

As the obsessive music starts we see her hand reach out – to strangle or caress? The abstract studio with its sloping wall and tall windows is reminiscent of the gabled attic on the cover of 'Lionheart' similarly oppressive. The two lovers/protagonists wear identical 'unisex' grey clothes, the beautiful skirt-like trousers based on the ceremonial 'hakama' worn for the martial arts of Aikido and Kendo. The concentration of dancers and viewers is enhanced by the absence of 'singing'. It is, in effect, a ballet.

The movements are tremendously demanding and difficult, but graceful. There are images of crucifixion and of one person passing through another and becoming the other, the cutting perfectly complementing the choreography. A simple but moving effect is where Kate is flung down and rises like her own soul out of her body to continue the struggle. The camera-work also heightens the disturbing sensation of drowning in a sea of people and the schizoid fear of a crowd all with one face.

The surreal scenery of impossible corridors in space and an endless road are neither theatre nor location. Kate is very keen on corridors in these later videos. They have the claustrophobic feel of tunnels – Kafka-esque corridors of power in labyrinthine ministry buildings. They are essentially cinematic scenery where a camera can follow but not an audience. Finally we are back in the tall studio as the couple mime the repeated drawing of a bow – a merging of Cupid and Zen archery?

'Cloudbusting' is a location film, but an entirely different conception from the old promo clips. In effect what Kate is making here and in 'Experiment IV' is a silent movie, with the record providing both soundtrack and caption cards. Julian Doyle directed – "He was suggested to me by Terry Gilliam. Terry is one of my favourite film makers." (He directed *The Time Bandits* (1981) and *Brazil* (1985).)

Kate made the brilliant choice of Donald Sutherland as Daddy (Wilhelm Reich) – "I had this crazy idea of using a very tall actor to play the father and myself to appear as the small boy. We were lucky – we had a friend who made the contact for us. We sent in the script and I talked to him and he was very interested, which was fantastic! He just happened to have the four days we needed to shoot the video. It all seemed to come together so well and so quickly. He was our first choice. I'm a big fan of him as an actor and he really was perfect for the part – there couldn't have been anyone better. He looks so right."

And so, in consequence, does Kate as she clings to this tall figure. For the first time she is playing a character part, not another version of herself. Teena Earnshaw did the make-up and Anthony Yacomine made the short wig. Pamela Keats supplied the dungarees and wellios.

The film simply but graphically tells the (true) story. "The song was inspired by the book, 'A Book of Dreams' by Peter Reich which was such a strong magical story that the plot was there and the most difficult areas were trying to do the story and the characters justice." (We see the book in the father's pocket – a jokey, surreal touch.) Peter Reich has since heard the song and seen the video. "These were worrying moments for me – what if he didn't like it – if I'd got it wrong? But he said he found them very emotional and that I'd captured the situation. This was the ultimate reward for me." They stayed in touch – "We write to each other and I enjoy the contact very much."

1986

25th May 1986. Kate joins in *Sport Aid* mini-marathon at Blackheath, South London. Fellow celebrity runners included Glenda Jackson and Jools Holland.

16th June 1986. *The Hair Of The Hound* video EP released featuring the four videos for the *Hounds Of Love*.

20th October 1986. *Don't Give Up* single released by Peter Gabriel (featuring Kate in a duet).

23rd October 1986. Makes personal appearance at the Claude Gill Book shop in London's Oxford Street signing copies of the *Comic Relief* book with fellow stars of the show.

Julie Angel

Kate was worried about playing opposite such a good actor. "In 'Running Up That Hill' I was trying to act a dancer and they are facial expressions I know the sensations of, but playing a little boy opposite Donald I had a 90 per cent chance of looking a total idiot!" She need not have worried. "Donald made it seem extremely natural. He was just like my Dad, he could make it rain and I would watch him being taken away. I must say it was an extremely moving experience, burnt strongly into my memory up on the hill with the machine and the wind . . ."

The film 'soundtrack' is an extended version of the original record, with vocals between verses chanting, 'It's you and me, Daddy – it's you and me!' This cry is also heard on 'Running Up That Hill' and 'Burning Bridge', the B-side of the single 'Cloudbusting' where it becomes 'You and me against the world', which seems to be what Kate has in mind in all these songs.

The other star of the piece is the Cloudbuster machine which was designed by H.R. Giger who designed the film *Alien*. "It came out of our heads based on vague information from the book," Kate explained. "It had to look larger than life – elegant, strange, aimed at the sky. In its early stages I really wondered – four cardboard tubes on wheels – eek! But by the last stages on screen it looked superb." When last heard of it was resting in a garage not far from the farm!

'Hounds Of Love' tells a story. Not necessarily the lyric of the song, but a parallel story which conveys the same mood and message. It is a miniature B-movie and starts with the words of a British fifties film *The Night Of The Demon* (1957 *Curse Of The Demon* in the USA). Halliwell's book of films describes it as having "a strong Hitchcock flavour." 'It's in the trees – it's coming!'

This video combines the threatening mood of *Brazil* with the look and feel of old movies. "We wanted to suggest a piece of 'Hitchcock' – a short thriller. Paddy inspired me into a *Thirty-Nine Steps* theme and for the two to three weeks over Christmas (1985) my life became this third video." (*Thirty-Nine Steps* – Hitchcock 1935.)

1986

27th October 1986. *Experiment IV/ Wuthering Heights* (new vocal) single released to promote the forthcoming greatest hits compilation.

10th November 1986. *The Whole Story* compilation LP released including new track, *Experiment IV* and revised vocal on *Wuthering Heights*.

THE WHOLE STORY (compilation) (EMI) KBTVI

Side One
Wuthering Heights (new vocal)
Cloudbusting
The Man With The Child In His Eyes
Breathing
Wow
Hounds Of Love

Side Two
Running Up That Hill
Army Dreamers
Sat In Your Lap
Experiment IV(*)
The Dreaming
Babooshka

*(*Experiment IV* drums: Stuart Elliot, guitar: Alan Murphy, violin: Nigel Kennedy. Recorded Summer 1986.)

The early shot of a vast piston engine is reminiscent of *Modern Times* (Chaplin 1936) or *Metropolis* (Fritz Lang 1926). Here she opens the film dressed as a librarian – tweeds, spectacles and hair piled up in a chignon. Then just as she spots the 'men from the ministry' we glimpse a familiar portly figure in a bowler hat – Alfred Hitchcock's trademark was to make a moment's appearance as an extra in every film he directed and this was Kate's witty use of a lookalike. The film also brilliantly evokes a nightmare, fleeing through a forest, branches snatching at them, discarding clothes as they run. Kate's hair soon falls glamorously about her shoulders.

'The Big Sky' is witty and exuberant and "a lot of fun" to make. It is as full of visual *doubles entendres* as Kate's lyrics. The whole tone of this video is very Spielberg – we start with a misty backlit crowd out of *Close Encounters* (1977) then join Kate on a fantasy roofscape, all old tiles and brick chimneys reminiscent of *Peter Pan* or the first shots in *Pinocchio*. Kate is dressed in a kind of shiny test-pilot suit scanning the sky with binoculars. We see the most wonderful procession of sky-scapes – clouds rushing past like *Rumblefish*, storms, even a solar eclipse (all blue-screen superimposition effects).

In Kate's sky the moon becomes a searchlight hunting bomber planes, then it's a spotlight and we're down on a stage in the company of everyone who ever flew (Superman) or had their head in the clouds (giraffes). "We needed an avenue of people from the Wright Brothers to two astronauts to simulate aviation history." Everyone was there – Paddy on dijeridu, boyfriend Del in flying gear, and even brother Jay as an astronaut. There follows a whacky stomping finale performed to an audience of 200 Fan Club members.

'The Hair Of The Hound' video EP came out in June 86, then later that year EMI, not wanting to miss out on the tremendous upsurge in Kate's popularity, released 'The Whole Story' project – the first 'best of Kate Bush' album ('The Singles File' was not an album) together with a video. At first Kate was unhappy about this move. "I was concerned that it would be like a 'K-Tel' record, a cheapo combo with little thought behind it. (But) we put a lot of work into the packaging and running order and the

Photo: *Ben Elton, Kate and Stephen Fry signing copies of the Comic Relief book in London, 1986.*

response has been phenomenal – I'm amazed." The phenomenal response was 900,000 sales – triple platinum, outselling 'The Kick Inside'.

Kate had similar worries about the video compilation but worked hard to rush through the 'Experiment IV' film so there would be something new (and added the new 'Wow' video). She was enjoying rising to the challenge of directing ("Actually it was Experiment III") and decided to keep her own appearance on screen to a minimum so she could concentrate on this and "On being behind the camera which I really enjoy".

The cast included Dawn French, Hugh Laurie, Richard Vernon, Peter Vaughan (who played Mr Helpman in *Brazil*), Del in the dentist's chair, Paddy in the straitjacket and Jay, who is sitting behind the desk on the right as the Professor enters the building. "Paddy played the lunatic and in every take his sounds were just as impressive as his visuals – the crew were so impressed they applauded him!"

As in 'Cloudbusting' there is another 'star' in this video – the Thing! This monster was created by *Image Animation* who produced the wonderful array of devils for the recent cult movie *Hellraiser*. Director Bob Keen found a message from Kate on his answerphone asking him to get in touch (and he has kept this memento – wouldn't you?). His partner Geoff Portass is the supervising designer and Kate explained to him what she wanted over the phone. "It's a sound demon so it must have a large mouth to look as if it's screaming." Geoff did some sketches and he, Bob and assistant Roy Puddefoot took the designs along to East Wickham farm. They knocked on a big gate (beware of the dog). Bob, Geoff and Roy are all tall and when the gate opened they were surprised by the tiny figure who peered round it – Kate herself!

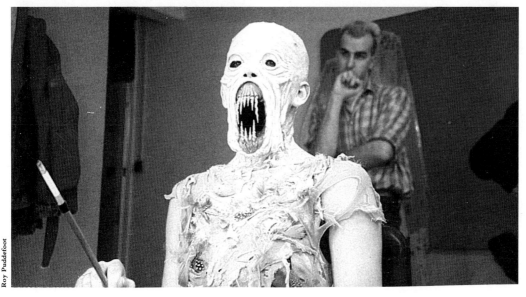
Roy Puddefoot

Left: Kate proves that smoking can seriously damage your health!

She didn't take them into the house but led them round the back to a rickety old barn. Behind the rough wooden door was a heavy steel door, and they stepped from the yard into a modern high-tech studio. (The heavy steel door is not so much for security as for sound-proofing.)

Kate led the way on through into a dinette sitting area with small kitchen. It was very unpretentious with rough blue plaster walls and homely wallpaper! She sat them down and made tea and took great interest in their work saying she wished she had got their job, it must be so fascinating.

Kate loved their designs and didn't want anything changed. "She knew what she wanted, but once she had explained something she never interfered. It was the same with everyone – in every department she got the best people in and then trusted them to do their best. Maybe if she hadn't liked something she would have said, but she always seemed happy."

What she was less happy about was having the life-cast made . . . "She made us tea and we covered her face in seaweed!" Alginate is pink rubbery stuff made from seaweed extract, and is used to make a mould of the face as the base for a mask. (Dentists also use it.) They covered her entire face and part of her ears, then she had to remain immobile for 20 minutes. She could just breathe through her nose. It's Roy's job to help people to breathe – he sits between their legs and keeps their nostrils clear. He threw Del out of the room because he was messing about and making her laugh: "Wey! – you're going under now!"

EB Gibson and 'Chesterfield' outside the granary store c.1902, which today houses Kate's own recording studio.

Bexley Local Studies Dept.

During the following week they made the Thing – a full mask for Kate to wear and a separate model based on a shop-window dummy. It all had to be done in a great hurry as the video was being included on 'The Whole Story' collection due for release before Christmas. There were a few problems, "The reason for the 'zits' on the monster's head is because Kate's hair is so long that when Teena (Earnshaw) put it up she used hair grips which showed up under the 'bald wig', so Geoff made them up to look like zits." Because of pressure of time the teeth were made out of 'bakeable' modelling clay, and it was hard to get a good smooth surface, so they tried a spiral appearance like unicorn horns. "Kate liked them – the whole project was very flukey like that, how well it turned out considering the pressure of time."

1986

The Whole Story
Kate's comments about each track:

Wuthering Heights
"It was a strange and exciting experience re-mixing and putting a new vocal to this song. When I first sang it in 1977 my voice was so different."

Cloudbusting
"I find it difficult to separate song from video. Sitting on Cloudbuster with the sun going down and working with Donald Sutherland are two experiences I will never forget."

The Man With The Child In His Eyes
"The earliest of all the tracks. I was 16 when it was recorded and terrified working with a large orchestra for the first time."

The Dreaming
"Whenever I hear this I can't help seeing Rolf Harris in the recording studio playing the didgeridoo and creating the Australian outback all around him. No one else could have been so good."

Hounds Of Love
"The hounds that appear on the album cover look soft and sleepy, but it took a lot of time before they settled down. They wrecked the set a few times . . ."

Breathing
"The world seemed to be heading for trouble when this was released. That hasn't changed."

Wow
"I had forgotten how beautiful the strings are on this track. Andrew Powell's arrangement is so moody."

Sat In Your Lap
"Shows the direction I began to go in at the time. It was my first solo production and we had a chance to really start experimenting with new areas."

Pictorial Press

Geoff and Roy came in on the final two days of a two-week shoot which was already over-running on time and budget. "Kate was knackered by this time. She was always up till two am and starting at six the next day."

The set was an old military hospital near Blackheath which was actually designed by Florence Nightingale. It was massive with enormous wards connected by endless corridors which ran from building to building. Most of it was peeling and crumbling but the parts used were thoroughly rewalled, floored and painted till it all looked like new. The place was rather eerie though. "We explored a bit – it was empty but there were still prayer books in the chapel."

Work began at four am and as this was November it was bitterly cold. Their first job was fitting Kate with a bald cap for the Siren, which is how she first appears. Then the blonde wig would fit on top. She was exhausted and dozed off while they were fitting it, just waking up every time the cold glue touched her skin. Then her regular make-up lady started and she dozed off completely, just waking up for the shot – "When she turned in a great performance!"

Kate started shooting at seven am and spent two hours leaning on a box looking ethereal. She only did close-up shots, wearing jeans but they were still shooting her at lunchtime. In the afternoon the stunt-woman Tracy wore the harness for the Siren flying shots. "Bob Harman did the wire work for the flying bits – he did the *Superman* movies."

It had been decided Kate wouldn't wear the mask for the Thing because of the time taken to put it on. "And although we'd left little holes in the eyes she could hardly see, let alone direct when wearing it."

Despite her exhaustion Kate was very alert when directing. Here again she trusted the actors to do their best. She would describe the situation then let them get on with it. They never saw her act something out for anyone. She was always present but she took very much a background role, almost diffident.

Everything seemed to take ages, as always when filming. Certain things ended up being rushed and had to be cut. There is a brief glimpse of the Thing coming out of its cocoon (a sheath of material) – it spreads its wings and you see the tail. But that was only on screen for a moment. (Charles Knode did the costume design – he also designed for the film *Legend*.)

There was a lot of hanging about in a trailer outside. It was too cold to wait around on set – the place was freezing. "Kate was wearing a pullover, a leather jacket and another pullover over the top – and she still looked gorgeous!" Because the hours were so long there were two firms doing the catering – "Fivestar who are the best around and another bunch who were crap. They were in filthy aprons serving Birds Eye mousse for afters!" So much for the glamour of the entertainment world!

They spent most of their time with Teena, Kate's make-up artist. Teena Earnshaw has been with Kate for years. She does all the videos. "When Kate does *Top Of The Pops* they book into the (Kensington) Hilton as she doesn't like the make-up people at the BBC. So she arrives at the studio fully made up. Kate fully trusts her." Teena is in her forties, quite plump and punky, jet black hair and wears very tight black skirts you'd expect to see on a younger thinner girl, but she looks great. She's ex-BBC.

At nine pm they were told, 'You've got to do this quickly', 50 minutes to put the mask on Tracy! Normally it would take three hours! The mask was filmed for two hours then at 11.30 it was the dummy head – made by Geoff and Roy. There's a shot of this rushing at the Professor's face. This was filmed in reverse as it would have been impossible to do without hitting him. And when it appears to swoop at the camera it's just someone jigging the model up and down while it's the camera that moves.

Another effect is where Dawn French and Prof Jerry Coe walk down the long corridor. It has an unreal, dream-like quality and in reality they are walking 'on the spot' on a camera-dolly (trolley) which is being towed down the corridor. Then they just turn and step off at the end.

1986

Experiment IV
"It's interesting to compare my first single with this later single. And it's remarkable that after nine years I am still working with the same drummer Stuart Elliot."

Running Up That Hill
"The first new track for almost three years and it was a very rewarding feeling when it was received so well."

Army Dreamers
"The earliest track to show the strong influence of traditional Irish music on my songs."

Babooshka
"I love the melody line of the bass guitar on this song. We got through a lot of boxes of broken crockery to get the right sound at the end – the canteen ladies were not impressed."

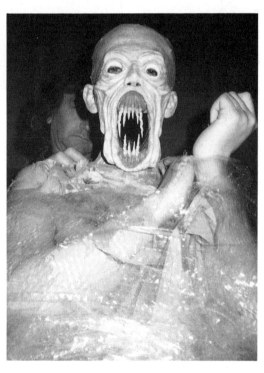

Roy Puddefoot

Left: *Sporting the costume she did not perform in for 'Experiment IV'.*

Below: *The alginate mask.*

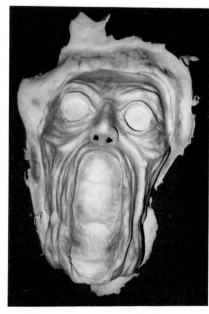

Roy Puddefoot

As soon as everything was over Kate rushed up and thanked them, shaking their hands with both hers, saying "I'm sorry! So sorry it went on so late!" Roy could only think, "She's the nicest pop star anyone could want to meet!"

'Experiment IV' was made as a B-movie, not a pop promo video. The single was already in the charts when it was filmed. It looks best on the big screen as a short film – it was shown with *Heartburn* and later *Castaway*, Nicolas Roeg's film for which Kate wrote 'Be Kind To My Mistakes'. "It must be played loud," said Geoff, confirming what Kate says on 'The Dreaming' – 'this album was made to be played loud.'

Maybe some of Kate's fans were disappointed that her appearance on screen was so brief but it is an important piece of Kate's work and was obviously a new area she was keen to explore. It is a fitting culmination to 'The Hair Of The Hound' project. Reflecting on the changes covered on *The Whole Story* video she said, "Visually I see a shift from being inspired by dance (Lindsay Kemp being a big influence) to filmic imagery (being influenced by all the films I love so much). I find the combination of film and music very exciting and it's very rare for people to concentrate on both with equal concern. But when it works it's so powerful – *The Wall, Singing In The Rain, Amadeus* – there are definitely people moving this way more and more – it's great!"

IN HER OWN WORDS

Pictorial Press

1987

28th March 1987. Kate appears at the 1987 Amnesty International concert at the Palladium, performing *Running Up That Hill* and *Let It Be* with Dave Gilmour.

May 1987. Kate records track called *This Woman's Work* for new John Hughes film *She's Having A Baby*. Film scheduled for release in early 1988.

1987 (Late). Kate agrees to lend her name to a new vegetarian campaign launched by the vegetarian society to publicise excessive cruelties within specific areas of the meat trade.

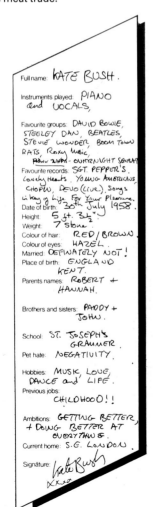

Full name: KATE BUSH.

Instruments played: PIANO and VOCALS,

Favourite groups: DAVID BOWIE, STEELEY DAN, BEATLES, STEVIE WONDER, BOOM TOWN RATS, Roxy Music, FRANK ZAPPA - OUTRIGHT SONLAT

Favourite records: SGT. PEPPER'S. Lonely Hearts, YOUNG AMERICANS, CHOPIN, DEVO (LIVE), Songs in Key of Life For Your Pleasure.

Date of birth: 30th July 1958.

Height: 5 ft. 3½"

Weight: 7 Stone.

Colour of hair: RED/BROWN.

Colour of eyes: HAZEL.

Married: DEFINATELY NOT!

Place of birth: ENGLAND KENT.

Parents names: ROBERT + HANNAH.

Brothers and sisters: PADDY + JOHN.

School: ST. JOSEPH'S GRAMMER.

Pet hate: NEGATIVITY.

Hobbies: MUSIC, LOVE, DANCE and LIFE.

Previous jobs: CHILDHOOD!!

Ambitions: GETTING BETTER, + DOING BETTER AT EVERYTHING.

Current home: S.E. LONDON

Signature: Kate Bush xxx

Record Mirror Questionnaire 1979.

"I much prefer to write lyrics than do an interview."

When we started this book we had to contend with the discouragement of knowing that Kate does not like being written about. But as we read books and interviews spanning the length of her career we soon came to realise why she mistrusts writers. After the initial burst of wonder and enthusiasm she was often treated shabbily, especially by the rock press. They soon came to dismiss her as a sexy female with a weird voice, and then when she started experimenting they were not prepared to take the trouble to understand what she was doing. (To be fair, journalists have very little time for this sort of in-depth assessment and much of Kate's work needs careful study.)

Not only did this affect the critics, it also spoiled a number of interviews. An interview can seldom rise above the tone of the questions asked and in some of them it is clear that Kate feels uncomfortable and has no scope to expand or explain.

"I find it very difficult to express myself in interviews," she says in *The Club* magazine (1987). "I feel I'm a song-writer, not a personality and I find it difficult to talk about my songs sometimes. In a way they speak for themselves and the subjects or inspirations can be so personal or just seem ridiculous when spoken about.

"Often people have so many preconceptions that I spend most of the interview trying to defend myself from the image that was created by the media eight years ago. (They) seem to dwell on this old 'me' and I find it disappointing when I want to talk about my current work . . . The interviews I've sat through sometimes hanging onto my patience with the skin of my teeth thinking it's good for my tolerance.

"There are good people to talk to . . . They make you think about areas you might not have even considered before."

When she meets a sympathetic interviewer who knows enough about her work to ask intelligent questions Kate shows she is very happy to talk. Her answers can be revealing, informative and often amusing.

Kate: "I think in a way that classical music is a superior form of music because it has so much space for the listeners to move around in. I love listening to classical music because I find it quite inspiring for my work. So maybe because I love these things so much I suppose they do tend to rub off on me. A lot of classical music is so good that it challenges you . . . It's not really copying but rather, wanting to produce that same kind of vibe. To try and get the same kind of atmosphere which that music creates when you listen to it." (PS 1985 (★))

"I think the first pop thing I ever heard which I really liked was 'Little Red Rooster' (The Rolling Stones). I heard it in a car coming back from the shops and I thought it fascinating . . . the fact that someone wasn't singing quite in tune and, because of that, was getting a very different emotion out of it." (PS 1985)

Kate: "I was always impressed by the words in folk songs. They're always stories, each song is a story – not like the lyrics of pop songs." (PS 1985)

"People are just full of songs. If you just sit down and talk to someone they come out with about four novels! I think most of my songs have been inspired by people and things people think about." (BBC 1979)

"I think you have to work on some of the words a bit, which isn't an easy thing to do from a listener's point of view. I think in so many ways that's what music is about. It's like in paintings – the artist can be drawing something incredibly deep and people look at it and just see splodges, but they like it. That's what really matters . . . it's your own personal interpretation and love of it. In many cases what the original artist meant doesn't come through, and I don't think it matters. But there's always a small percentage of people who do actually see what it's about. There's so many songs that I like but I doubt that I know what they really mean. In a way that's half the fun." (PN 1982)

"Right from the start I carried two or three musicians – Paddy, my brother. He's the one who allowed me to use unusual instruments because he was able to play them. Brian Bath and Del Palmer have both been with me since the KT Bush Band five years ago. I feel I would still want to use them in future which is great because they form a nucleus. But I would love to have a secure band because that's a very good feeling. They know what you want eventually and it must become easier to communicate." (1982)

Is it a kind of benevolent dictatorship in the studio where what you say goes and the musicians just take it? (Paddy fell about with laughter at this point.)

Kate: "Well, quite honestly I think it is sometimes. But I think in most cases I really do know what I want. There are never any serious problems 'cos the fellows I work with are great and I think they just find amusing all the things that I like and ask them to do. In a way, the most important thing for me, I feel, is if I can convey to them the *atmosphere* of the song, the sort of feeling which I want them to produce. Then I feel that they will give me what I want, as long as they're in tune with the song on the same level. I spend an awful lot of time trying to explain the story and the atmosphere and all that sort of thing." (PS 1985)

1988

March 1988. Release date for the new LP is put back. Although the new record was said to be progressing well, no new release date was announced.

30th July 1988. Kate celebrates her 30th birthday.

Julie Angel

Photos: *High flyer Paddy Bush in The Big Sky.*

Paddy: "To cultivate music you have to spend a lot of time *by yourself* making a lot of very strange sounds over and over again . . . When there's a family all in one house and you're getting your music together normally the others in the family close the doors and try to keep the sounds out." (PS 1985)

1988

Sept 1988. 'Answers to Nothing' LP released by Midge Ure featuring track 'Sister And Brother'; Kate on backing vocals.

Below: *At Elstree for 'The Big Sky' video shoot.*

Julie Angel

"Lead vocals require the right feeling and atmosphere, mentally and in the studio. The hardest thing is being psyched up in the right way to do the vocal with the right emotional feeling. The hardest thing for me is to be able to feel relaxed enough to be uninhibited. I like to do them with Del because I feel much more relaxed than if there's an outside engineer there. I become quite sensitive when I start singing." (PS 1985)

"We do work in a very isolated way – you know, most of the time it's just three of us in the control room: the engineer, Del and myself, say. And then suddenly to go out into the world to do promotion is quite a culture shock. There are really a lot of people out there, and to walk into a room with perhaps a few hundred people in it and they're all looking at you – it's a very different world!" (PS 1985)

Is isolation essential to your creative feelings?

"Yes, absolutely. They're two very separate things, two different energies, and I can only really concentrate if that's all I have to do. If there's other things to do besides make an album they just become distractions." (RB 1985)

"I think you have to recognise a point where things are as good as they can be within the limitations before they start going off again. It's definitely a peak and then it can go off. So you have to recognise where more effort will make it better, but when to stop.

"It's almost like the music itself dictates it. When a track is sounding right, when it's ready, you can just feel it. Then you mix it – that's when you play with all the little raw edges. You just know when everything's finished." (RB 1985)

"It takes me a long while to come out of the wake of one album and into the energy of a new album. You go from one very intense atmosphere into another one, and you've got to get some new inspiration in between." (PS 1985)

"I think it's important that each album *should* be different – otherwise you're not going anywhere and exploring but staying in a rut." (PS 1985)

Do songs come easily?

"No, some do, but the majority I have to work for very hard and it's extremely frustrating, but it's worth it to get something in the end. Something I got hooked on quite young, just playing with the piano – the whole excitement of creating something out of nothing." (RB 1985)

"It's getting harder for me to write. I think the longer I'm around the harder it is for me to find something convincing in my art. There are all kinds of subject matters which I think I could probably have enjoyed at an earlier time but which now I find trivial. So there are all these changes. You know, the more you see the more there is to fear, and the more there is to fear the more there is to learn. And I think that very much applies to my work." (PS 1985)

Interviews are fascinating and often revealing, but it is through her music that we really come to know her. Kate Bush is a private person, but one who is prepared to share her secrets. Her songs represent a very personal document of thoughts, emotions, people and situations. Drawing her initial stimulus from outside, she uses highly developed writing and recording methods to explore herself, then fearlessly offers the results to public scrutiny. This delicate and demanding process of self-analysis requires great concentration, and hence isolation and privacy.

Inevitably after working for long periods of time in these intense conditions she takes time to adjust to the normal rough and tumble of the social world. But she is not by nature a recluse, nor is she over-serious. She has great zest for life and her work displays constant energy and humour. It is clear from the significance her self-revelations have to so many people that she is not out of touch with people and their concerns.

Do you ever write a song then decide it is too intimate, too personal, too compromising perhaps to offer to the public?

"No, that's never happened yet. The only reason a song will get dropped is if it is not good enough. If it was good enough it would go on." (PS 1985)

Through her tireless efforts Kate has made it possible for us to know her, and to know her better than we know some of our close friends, better sometimes than we know ourselves.

((*)These quotes are drawn from several interviews. PS is Peter Swale, RB: Robert Brown, PN: Peter Nash of the *Daily Mirror* plus an unattributed picture disc.)

The new single from Kate Bush

The Man With The Child In His Eyes EMI 2806

THE DISCOGRAPHY/ GENERAL LISTINGS

SINGLES/EPs

1 Wuthering Heights/Kite EMI 2719
2 The Man With The Child In His Eyes/ Moving EMI 2806
3 Hammer Horror/Coffee Homeground EMI 2887
4 Wow/Fullhouse EMI 2911
5 Kate Bush On Stage EP – Them Heavy People/ Don't Push Your Foot On The Heartbrake/ James And The Cold Gun/L'Amour Looks Something Like You.
(Double pack single in gatefold sleeve – also released as 12" disc) EMI MIEP 2991
6 Breathing/The Empty Bullring EMI 5058
7 Babooshka/Ran Tan Waltz EMI 5085
8 Army Dreamers/Delius/Passing Through Air EMI 5106
9 December Will Be Magic Again/ Warm And Soothing EMI 5121
10 Sat In Your Lap/Lord Of The Reedy River EMI 5201
11 The Dreaming/Dreamtime (instrumental) EMI 5350
12 There Goes A Tenner/ Ne T'Enfuis Pas EMI 5350
13 Wuthering Heights/The Man With The Child In His Eyes Old Gold OG 9380
14 The Singles File – Boxed set of 11 of Kate's singles, the **On Stage** EP and **Ne T'Enfuis Pas/ Un Baiser D'Enfant** and booklet.
15 Running Up That Hill (A Deal With God)/ Under The Ivy EMI KB1
Running Up That Hill (A Deal With God) (Extended Remix)/**Under The Ivy/Running Up That Hill** (instrumental) 12" single EMI 12 KB1
16 Cloudbusting/Burning Bridges EMI KB2
Cloudbusting (Organon Mix)/ **Burning Bridges/My Lagan Love** 12" single EMI 12 KB2
17 Hounds Of Love/The Handsome Cabin Boy EMI KB3
Alternative **Hounds Of Love/Jig Of Life/ The Handsome Cabin Boy** 12" single EMI 12 KB3
18 The Big Sky (special single mix)/ **Not This Time** EMI KB4
The Big Sky (Meteorological Mix)/ **Not This Time/The Morning Fog** 12" single EMI 12 KB4
19 Experiment IV/Wuthering Heights EMI KB5
Experiment IV (12" remix)/ **Wuthering Heights** (new vocal)/ **20 December Will Be Magic Again** EMI 12 KB5

ALBUMS

1 The Kick Inside EMI EMC 3223
2 Lionheart EMI EMA 787
The Kick Inside (picture disc) EMI EMPC 3223
3 Never For Ever EMI EMA 794
4 The Dreaming EMI EMC 3419
Lionheart (reissue) Fame FA 41 3094 1
5 Hounds Of Love EMI KAB 1
6 The Whole Story EMI KBTV1
7 Kate Bush I (UK) BAK 2006
(Unofficial picture disc 1985)
8 Kate Bush II (UK) BAK 2073
(Unofficial picture disc 1982)
9 BBC Transcription LP

VARIOUS FOREIGN OFFICIAL LP AND SINGLE RELEASES

We could add to infinitum lists of official promotional discs, variations of picture disc covers, Polish 'postcard' singles, one sided singles etc. Suffice to say there are plenty of very collectable official releases from around the world. Kate has become one of the most collectable UK artists on the scene and records and memorabilia change hands at considerable prices. Below is a brief list of items which fall slightly outside the above category and are more sought after by collectors.

Ne T'Enfuis Pas/Un Baiser D'Enfant (released in France and Canada). Pathe Marconi EMI 5444
Un Baiser D'Enfant/Suspended In Gaffa EMI America 72931 (Canada)
Ne T'Enfuis Pas/Dreamtime EMI America 72917 (Canada)
An Interview With Kate Bush (Canadian Promo LP) EMI America SPRO 282
The Early Years (East German LP. Withdrawn prior to release).
Sat In Your Lap single released in Eire.
Self Portrait (US Promo LP).
EMI America SSA 3024
Hounds Of Love (US release on grey marbled vinyl and pink vinyl).
Sat In Your Lap (Canadian mini LP, issued on clear, brown, blue, white, green and red vinyl). EMI America.
The Dreaming (four track US promo EP).
Kate Bush (mini LP) (US release).
Sat In Your Lap/James And The Cold Gun/ Babooshka/Suspended In Gaffa/ Un Baiser D'Enfant EMI America MLP 19004
Kate Bush (mini LP) (Canadian release) **Sat In Your Lap/James And The Cold Gun/ Ne T'Enfuis Pas/Babooshka/ Suspended In Gaffa/Un Baiser D'Enfant.** EMI America (Canada) 19004

COMPACT DISCS

1 The Kick Inside EMI CDP 74060122
2 Lionheart EMI CDP 7460652
3 Never For Ever EMI CDP 7463602
4 The Dreaming EMI CDP 7463612
5 Hounds Of Love EMI CDP 7461642
6 The Whole Story (compilation) EMI CDP 7464142
7 Kate Bush III – Picture Disc CD Interview CBAK 4011

VIDEOS

Kate Bush Live At The Hammersmith Odeon
Edited live footage of Kate's Hammersmith Odeon concert – 13/5/79
Moving/Them Heavy People/Violin/Strange Phenomena/Hammer Horror/Don't Push Your Foot On The Heartbreak/Wow/Feel It/Kite/James And The Cold Gun/Oh England My Lionheart/Wuthering Heights.
Directed by Keef Macmillan.
VHS TVD 90 0503 2
Kate Bush – The Singles File
Tape features: **Wuthering Heights/The Man With The Child In His Eyes/Hammer Horror/Wow/Them Heavy People/Breathing/Babooshka/Army Dreamers/Sat In Your Lap/The Dreaming/ Suspended In Gaffa/There Goes A Tenner.**
Videos directed by Keef Macmillan, Brian Wiseman and Paul Henry.
VHS TVE 90 1430 2
Kate Bush – The Hair Of The Hound
Running Up That Hill/Hounds Of Love/The Big Sky/ Cloudbusting (final track features different mix and slightly different vocal to singles).
Videos directed by Kate, David Garfath and Julian Doyle.
VHS MVR 99 0053 2
Kate Bush – The Whole Story
Wuthering Heights/Cloudbusting/The Man With The Child In His Eyes/Breathing/Wow/Hounds Of Love/Running Up That Hill/Army Dreamers/Sat In Your Lap/Experiment IV/The Dreaming/Babooshka/ The Big Sky.
Directed by Kate, Keef Macmillan, Brian Wiseman, Paul Henry, David Garfath and Julian Doyle.
VHS MVP 99 1143 2

The Comic Relief Utterly Utterly Rude Video Live
Features Kate singing **Breathing** and a comedy duet **Do Bears** with Rowan Atkinson.
VHS Virgin Video
The Secret Policeman's Third Ball
Kate sings **Running Up That Hill** and **Let It Be** with Dave Gilmour.
VHS
CV Peter Gabriel
Collection of videos from Peter Gabriel featuring two versions of the Gabriel/Bush duet **Don't Give Up.**
VHS

RELATED LP AND SINGLE RELEASES

Sing Children Sing Single release featuring Kate, Pete Townshend, Joe Brown and others. Charity record for UN Year Of The Child fund. (1979) CBS 8061
Peter Gabriel III Third solo Gabriel LP featuring Kate on two tracks, **Games Without Frontiers** and **No Self Control.** (Backing vocals.) (1980) Charisma CB 354
Unknown Soldier Roy Harper. LP featuring Kate on backing vocals on **You (The Game Part III).** (1980) Harvest SHVL 820
Flowers Zaine Griff. Single dedicated to Lindsay Kemp featuring Kate on vocals. Track also features on Griff's LP **Figures.** (1982) Polydor POLO 5061
Them Heavy People Ray Shell. Kate contributes backing vocals to her own song. (1981) EMI 5142
Seer Kate contributes backing vocals to the title track on this LP by Big Country. (1986) Phonogram MERH 87
The King Is Dead Kate again contributes backing vocals, this time on a Go West single. (1986) Chrysalis GOW6. This track also features on the Go West LP, **Dancing On The Couch.**
Utterly Utterly Live At The Shaftesbury Theatre Comic Relief LP features Kate with Rowan Atkinson, **Do Bears** and **Breathing.** (1986) WEA WX 51 (240 932)
The Secret Policeman's Third Ball Kate features on this Amnesty International LP release performing **Running Up That Hill** backed by the new Pink Floyd.
Let It Be Kate features on Ferry Aid's fund raising single.
Don't Give Up Kate Bush and Peter Gabriel duet taken from Gabriel LP **So.** (Released on 7" and 12" singles.) (1986) Charisma/Virgin PG5
Answers To Nothing Midge Ure LP featuring Kate on backing vocals on **Sister And Brother** (1988) Chrysalis.

MISCELLANEOUS TRACKS (FILMS)

The Magician. Written for **The Magician Of Lublin.** (This film has only been released on video.)
Be Kind To My Mistakes. Written for the soundtrack of Nicolas Roeg's **Castaway.**
This Woman's Work. Written for the soundtrack of **She's Having A Baby** directed by John Hughes.
Brazil. Cover version of the original song by Kate for the film of the same name. Directed by Kate's friend Terry Gilliam.

COMPILATION LPs FEATURING KATE

Hits Of The '70s (Reader's Digest 6 LP set) features **Wuthering Heights.**
Always And Forever includes **The Man With The Child In His Eyes.**
The Greatest Love includes **Wuthering Heights** (original version).
The Greenpeace Album includes **Breathing** compilation LP compiled by the Greenpeace charity.
The Prince's Trust Album includes Kate singing a live version of **Wedding List.**
Now That's What I Call Music 8 features **Running Up That Hill.**
Now That's What I Call Music 10 features **Don't Give Up.**
Hits Hits Hits 5 features **Hounds Of Love.**
Let's Hear It For The Girls features **Cloudbusting.**

BOOKS

Kate Bush – Words And Music From 'The Kick Inside'.
Featuring seven songs from the LP.
(EMI Music Publishing Ltd.) (1978.)

Kate Bush – Lionheart.
Complete music and lyrics from the LP. (Illustrated.) (EMI Music Publishing Ltd.) (1979.)
Kate Bush Biography. Subtitled 'Kate Bush – Princess of Suburbia'. Fred and Judy Vermorel. The first biographical Kate Bush book. In depth interviews with Kate's old school friends, local history etc. (Illustrated.) (Target Books.) (1980.)
Kate Bush – An Illustrated Biography. Paul Kerton. Well researched, featuring various interviews with people involved with Kate's rise and rise. (Illustrated.) (Proteus.) (1980.)
The Best Of Kate Bush.
Features 13 songs from the first three LPs with introduction and brief comments on each song by Kate. (Colour and black and white illustrations.) (EMI Music Publishing Ltd.) (1981.)
The Secret History Of Kate Bush (And The Strange Art Of Pop). Fred Vermorel.
Fred Vermorel's second attempt at tackling the history of Kate and, in far more detail, her family history. As a work of local history the book is invaluable and, had it not been for the brief association with Kate Bush, would probably have gone unpublished. Interesting selection of illustrations and interview material with EMI staff. Although put down by the Bush family and fans alike, it remains in print and the best selling Bush book to-date. (Omnibus Press.) (1983.)
Kate Bush – Hounds Of Love.
Containing complete music from the LP. (Black and white photos and colour poster.) (EMI Music Publishing Ltd.) (1985.)
Kate Bush – The Whole Story.
Complete listing from the LP. (EMI Music Publishing Ltd/International Music Publications.) (1987.)
Kate Bush.
Eight tracks with lyrics. (IMP Right Price.) (1987.)
Kate Bush Complete.
Accompanying book to 'The Whole Story' LP and video series. Book features chronology, discography, videography, music and lyrics to songs 1978-86. (Black and white illustrations.) (EMI Music Publishing Ltd/IMP.) (1987.)
Cathy.
Beautifully prepared collection of photographs taken by John Carder Bush of his sister through childhood. With a carefully written commentary and sepia toned pictures. (Available by post only. See Useful Contact Points.)

BOOTLEGS

As with any popular artist, Kate Bush bootlegs are a part of the 'must have everything' collectors list. In comparison with other major music figures, Kate has done very little live work, accordingly most bootlegs take the shape of live recordings from the Tour Of Life 1979 tour. Often albums are re-packaged and appear on different coloured vinyls but we have simply listed a cross-section of the most well known and collectable illegal records. None of the live recordings are particularly well made, officially released live material is naturally far superior.

Wow. (USA) 1983 Double LP set. Record One is the Hammersmith Odeon soundtrack. Record Two is from Kate's BBC TV special, both recordings from 1979. This was the first marketed Kate Bush bootleg.
Kate Bush Live In Europe. A triple LP set made up from live and studio recordings, mostly culled from European television appearances.
Secret Message. Japanese flexi-disc from the *Lionheart* magazine. As well as the emotional 'Let It Be' live recording from the Bill Duffield benefit concert it also contains messages from Kate and brother John. Also available on vinyl.
Kate Bush Live in Paris. Double LP set, live material as included in 'Live In Europe'.
A Bird In The Hand. Single LP release of selected tracks from the Hammersmith Odeon soundtrack.
Kate Bush – The Early Years. Hard to find West German disc of Kate's early Dave Gilmour demos recorded around 1973.
Moving. A re-issue of 'Live In Europe' in impressive packaging and also released as picture disc.
Kate Bush Under The Ivy Bush. German television recordings and demos from 1980 and '85. Attractive packaging. Single LP release.
Kate Bush Interview. Interview with Kate taken from the official 1985 Canadian interview LP. (7" disc.) Record also available as a 7" picture disc.
Phenomenon. Single LP recording of the Bristol Tour Of Life show.
Kate Bush Live In Manchester April 10th 1979. Yet another bootleg from the tour.
Passing Through The Air. Mixture of pirated B-sides and live recordings. (Features 'Wedding List' recorded at 1982 Prince's Trust concert, Kate backed

by all star line-up, Pete Townshend, Midge Ure, Phil Collins, Mick Karn and Gary Brooker).
Babooshka photograph picture disc. Interview with Kate from Sky satellite channel *Music Box*.
Kate Bush Live In Bristol England 1979. Another double LP from America in a well prepared fold-out cover.
Dreamtime – Kate Bush Live At The London Palladium 1979. Three LP set which speaks for itself. The whole show is faithfully recorded but, as with

most of Kate's live unofficial recordings, isn't particularly audible.
What Katie Did For Amnesty International. Kate and Dave Gilmour recorded at The Secret Policeman's Third Ball in 1987.
If You Could See Me Fly. Live material from the May 1979 Bill Duffield benefit concert.
Kate Bush – Temple Of Truth. Collection of live tracks on a single LP.

MISCELLANEOUS LISTS AND TRIVIA

Now we are really down to trivia! In compiling this book we have noticed various odd facts and incidental curiosities. The lists that follow are an attempt to present these in some sort of order.

FIRSTS

Song:'The Man With The Child In His Eyes' (written at age 14 and later recorded commercially)
Gig: the Rose of Lee pub in Lewisham with the KT Bush Band – April 1977
Interview: Capital Radio with Tony Myatt – 20 Jan 1978
Television appearance: *Bio's Bahnhof* in Germany – Feb 9 1978 *Top Of The Pops* – Feb 16 1978
Phone-in programme: *Personal Call* on Radio One – Feb 27 1979
Number one album: 'Never For Ever' (and first by any British solo female artist)
Midem Video Awards: 'Babooshka' won Best International Production and Best International Performance (first time these awards were given)
Self-produced album: 'The Dreaming'
Album from farm studio: 'Hounds Of Love'
Self-directed video: 'Hounds Of Love'
12-inch single: 'Running Up That Hill'

'ONES THAT GOT AWAY'

Jun 1977 'Maybe' – demoed and mastered but never released
Apr 1979 'Oh To Be In Love' – only track from first two albums not done on tour
May 1979 Invited to write and sing theme song for Bond film *Moonraker*
Nov 1980 'Ibiza' recorded with Peter Gabriel but never released
May 1981 Invited to play the Wicked Witch in Children's TV *Worzel Gummidge*
Jan 1982 Offered leading role in *Pirates Of Penzance* in West End theatre
May 1983 Kate's book *Leaving My Tracks* shelved
Aug 1983 'Ne T'Enfuis Pas'/'Un Baiser D'Enfant' single never released in Britain
1985 Cover version of 'Brazil' for Terry Gilliam's film never issued
Feb 1986 Plans to film 'The Ninth Wave' abandoned
America – the only major territory where Kate is not successful

THE SINGLES(*) | Chart Position

1	Wuthering Heights	1
2	Running Up That Hill	3
3	Babooshka	5
4	The Man With The Child In His Eyes	6
5	Them Heavy People (Live EP)	10
6	Sat In Your Lap	11
7	Wow	14
8	Army Dreamers	16
9	Breathing	16
10	The Hounds Of Love	18
11	Cloudbusting	20
12	Experiment IV	23
13	December Will Be Magic Again	29
14	The Big Sky	37
15	Hammer Horror	44
16	The Dreaming	48
17	There Goes A Tenner	–

THE ALBUMS(*)

1	The Whole Story Triple Platinum	1
2	The Kick Inside Triple Platinum	3
3	Hounds Of Love Double Platinum	1
4	Never For Ever Platinum	1
5	The Dreaming Gold	3
6	Lionheart Gold	6

(*)These two lists of records are informal, compiled from BMRB chart positions.

FAVOURITE ARTISTS etc (from record choices, interviews, etc)

J M Barrie
The Beatles
Captain Beefheart
David Bowie
Frederick Delius
Donovan
Bob Dylan
Bryan Ferry
Peter Gabriel
Roy Harper
Rolf Harris
Billie Holiday
Buddy Holly
Elton John
Lindsay Kemp
John Lennon
Lotte Lenya
Albert Lloyd
Kate and Anna McGarrigle
Joni Mitchell
Steely Dan
Oscar Wilde
Frank Zappa

'ONE AND ONLY'S'

1978 Only ad: in Japan Kate advertised Seiko watches
1979 The Tour Of Life was Kate's only tour
1980 'Night Scented Stock' – only wordless vocal track
'December Will Be Magic Again' – only single to have no video or be included on any album.
'Never For Ever' – only LP with no title track.
1981 'Lord Of The Reedy River' – only non-original non-traditional song covered
1982 'Dreamtime' – only true instrumental
'There Goes A Tenner' – only single never to chart
'Suspended In Gaffa' – only video for non-British single
1985 'My Lagan Love' – only unaccompanied vocal
1986 'Wow' – only track with two different videos issued on compilations

LIKES

Chocolate
Tea
Science fiction
Reading
Cinema
Television
Doing session work on other people's albums
Cats
Folk music
Greenpeace
Donald Sutherland
Terry Gilliam
The Young Ones

AND DISLIKES

Wasting time
Flying
Eating animals
Books about Kate Bush!

The International KATE BUSH Fanzine Summer 88

ENGLISH

WELSH

DUTCH

USEFUL CONTACTS

First stop for all Kate Bush fans has to be the official Kate Bush Fan Club. Practically into its tenth year of publication, the club's glossy colour magazine is one of the best official fan club publications for any artist. With regular contributions from Kate, brothers Paddy and John and many others closely associated with Kate, it carries all the major news with excellent quality photographs.

In early 1982, the first issue of *Homeground, The International Kate Bush Fanzine* was published. Quickly the fanzine established itself as a centre-piece for fan involvement and the sincerity of their work encouraged Kate to involve them with official club meetings. *Homeground*, run by Peter and Krystyna Fitzgerald-Morris and David Cross is now past its 30th issue and growing in quality and strength.

We have listed a number of current Kate Bush-inspired fanzines from around the world. As with any major artist, Kate has inspired many of her fans to write and draw their own interpretations to her work through her sheer originality. Listed is a cross-section of those fanzines. Do remember to enclose SAEs or IRCs when replying as fanzine and fan club funds are normally very low.

OFFICIAL SERVICE

The Official Kate Bush Fan Club.
Est.1979. Available from: PO Box 120, Welling, Kent DA16 3DS. The club is run by Lisa Bradley.

Information regarding the limited edition publication of *Cathy* is available from: **Kindlight**, PO Box 30, Welling, Kent DA16 3DL.

FANZINES

Homeground – semi-official magazine service. Est.1982. Available from: PO Box 176, Orpington, Kent BR5 3NA.
Cariad Kate – Welsh fanzine. Est.1987. Available from: 28 Millbrook Street, Plasmarl, Swansea.
Dreamtime – the Australian Kate Bush Magazine. Est.1984. Available from: 46 Gladstone Avenue, South Perth, 6151, Western Australia.
Lionheart – the magazine of the Japanese Fan Club. Est.1987. Available from: 5-6-14 Shimomeguro Meguro Ku Tokyo 153, Japan.
Watching Storms. Est.1987. Available from: 167 Central Avenue, East Prov, RI 02914, USA.
Still Breathing. Est.1988. Available from: 11588-72nd Avenue, Delta, British Columbia, V4E 1Z1, Canada.
N'Abandonne Pas – Kate Bush and Peter Gabriel fanzine. Est.1987. Available from: BP 389, 75962 Paris, Cedex 20, France.
Kate – the Dutch Fan Club. Available from: Postbus 2177, 4800 CD, Breda, The Netherlands.

AUSTRALIAN

KATE BUSH CONVENTION

April 85

ENGLISH

30th November 1985

UK

THE AUTHORS

Rikki Beadle-Blair

Ian Armstrong

SEAN MAYES

In 1967 Sean Mayes left Cambridge with a degree in philosophy and joined a rock 'n' roll band on piano. Fumble made three LPs, toured Europe and America with Bill Haley, Fats Domino and David Bowie and featured in the original cast of *Elvis* at the Astoria Theatre.

He then joined Bowie's band for a 1978 World Tour and can be heard on 'Stage' and 'Lodger'.

In 1983 he joined Tom Robinson for 'War Baby', touring and further LP tracks.

His last and liveliest band was Boysie, and his most recent venture was 'Wild At Heart' at London's Riverside Studios, described in *You* magazine as an 'all-singing-dancing-swearing show'.

KEVIN CANN

Born in Hackney, London, Kevin Cann trained as a designer in the UK and Singapore. He wrote the successful *David Bowie – A Chronology*, published in 1983; co-authored *The Starzone Interviews* in 1985 and was a contributing editor on *Starzone* magazine from 1981 to 1986.

In recent years he has worked with Adam Ant, Heaven 17, Visage, Brian Eno and Bill Nelson. In 1987 Kevin organised the first UK retrospective of work by the late watercolour artist Peter Schmidt. He has also worked as researcher for radio projects with Stage Broadcasts and Radio One.

The following books were an invaluable assistance to the authors: *Kate Bush – Princess Of Suburbia* by Fred Vermorel (Target Books), *Kate Bush – An Illustrated Biography* by Paul Kerton (Proteus), *Cathy* by John Carder Bush (Kindlight), *The Secret History Of Kate Bush (And The Strange Art Of Pop)* by Fred and Judy Vermorel (Omnibus Press), *Kate Bush Complete* (EMI Music Publishing Ltd), *The Best Of Kate Bush* (EMI Music Publishing Ltd), *The Gurdjieff Inheritance* by JH Reyner (Turnstone Press Ltd), Brewer's *Dictionary Of Phrase And Fable* (Cassell), *Guinness Book Of British Hit Singles* (Grrr Books Ltd), Halliwell's *Filmgoer's Companion* (Paladin), *A New Dictionary Of Music* by Arthur Jacobs (Penguin).